BALI'S EMBRACE: A LOVE STORY IN PARADISE

SHIBJIT MITRA

BlueRose ONE.com DIY
Stories Matter
NewDelhi • London

BLUEROSE PUBLISHERS
India | U.K.

For permissions requests or inquiries regarding this publication, please contact:

BLUEROSE PUBLISHERS
www.BlueRoseONE.com
info@bluerosepublishers.com
+91 8882 898 898
+4407342408967

ISBN: 978-93-6783-328-5

First Edition: January 2025

Contents

Acknowledgement

This book is a journey—both across landscapes and within myself. It is the culmination of countless miles, fleeting moments, and the profound impact of exploration. It is my humble attempt to capture the world as I've seen it, to relive the laughter, lessons, and awe of wandering paths both well-trodden and untouched.

Above all, this work is a testament to the people who have shaped me as much as any place I've visited. To my wife, Krittika, whose unwavering belief in me has been my greatest compass. To my mother, whose wisdom and love have grounded me. And to my father, whose support has been the steady foundation upon which I have always relied—I owe you more than words can express.

May this book inspire you, dear reader, to embark on your own journeys, to step out of the familiar and into the unknown, and to find your own stories in the world's vast tapestry.

Let's explore.

Preface

This book is not just a recollection of our travels; it is a heartfelt tapestry woven with the threads of love, discovery, and transformation. At its heart lies Bali—a land where ancient traditions merge seamlessly with nature's breathtaking beauty, where every temple has a story, every wave a rhythm, and every sunrise a blessing.

Our journey began with a dream—to step away from the ordinary and into a world that would awaken our senses and deepen our bond as a newly married couple. Bali was more than a destination for our honeymoon; it became the setting for a transformative adventure. From the mystical dawn at Tanah Lot Temple to the rugged cliffs of Uluwatu and the serene, turquoise waters of Nusa Penida, every moment unfolded like the pages of a storybook we were privileged to write.

The island welcomed us not as tourists but as part of its living tapestry, inviting us to understand its soul through its culture, people, and landscapes. We were humbled by the quiet devotion at its temples, mesmerized by the artistry of its dances, and rejuvenated by the healing stillness of its natural wonders. Each chapter of this book is a testament to the profound connection between humans and the world around them—a reminder that travel is as much about exploring within as it is about wandering afar.

Bali taught us the art of slowing down, of being present in the moment. It whispered to us through the crash of waves, the rustling of leaves, and the smiles of its people. It showed us that true beauty lies not just in majestic views but in the fleeting, quiet moments—an offering left at a shrine, the giggle of a child at a waterfall, or the shimmering light of dawn breaking over a volcano.

This book is a tribute to Bali and to the profound impact it had on us. It is a chronicle of our adventures and a glimpse into the joy, challenges, and wonders of a shared journey. More importantly, it is an invitation to you, dear reader, to embark on your own explorations—to seek the unknown, embrace the unexpected, and allow the world to shape and inspire you.

May these pages fill you with the same sense of awe and curiosity we felt as we discovered Bali. Let them remind you that the world is vast, beautiful, and waiting for your story to unfold. Let us take you to the edge of cliffs, the heart of jungles, and the soul of an island that forever etched itself into our hearts.

Welcome to our journey. Let's explore, dream, and wander together.

Our Adventure in Bali

A Journey Through Bali's Sacred Dream

The night unfolds in stillness, soft and deep,
A canvas painted with the stars' embrace.
Through quiet streets where ancient spirits sleep,
Our steps align with Bali's timeless grace.

The temple gates, in misty morning's hue,
Stand tall against the waves' eternal roar.
Each crashing crest, a hymn both old and new,
Invites the soul to wander and explore.

In verdant fields where rice terraces gleam,
And waterfalls cascade in whispered song,
The heart awakens to a living dream,
A world of peace where spirits all belong.

Through sacred paths and nature's vast expanse,
We find ourselves in Bali's mystic dance.

\- *Krittika Banerjee*

Chapter 1: The Journey Begins

March 6, 2024

The night at Kolkata Airport was calm and quiet, with only a few travellers moving slowly through the dimly lit terminal. Unlike the usual daytime hustle, the airport seemed to settle into a gentle rhythm, as if taking a deep breath along with us. Soft, warm lighting reflected off the polished floors, and the faint hum of overhead announcements filled the silence, sounding distant and almost soothing at this hour. Rows of empty chairs stretched out across the departure area, while a few people here and there dozed with heads tilted back, their bags tucked close to their sides.

We sipped warm tea from paper cups, feeling its gentle heat in our hands as we waited for our flight's boarding announcement. Outside, through the large glass windows, the quiet tarmac glowed under the soft orange lights. Planes were parked in a neat line, some with flashing blue and red lights on their tails, adding subtle glimmers to the otherwise muted scene. Occasionally, ground staff walked by with a purposeful yet relaxed stride, almost as if the world had slowed down in tandem with the night.

We found comfort in the stillness, sharing a few whispers and occasional smiles as we took in the tranquil atmosphere. It felt as if we were in a small cocoon, protected by the peacefulness around us, ready to launch ourselves into the next part of our journey. As the boarding time approached, the faint excitement of our upcoming adventure mingled with the night's calmness, giving us a moment to breathe, reflect, and embrace the beginning of a new chapter.

As dawn broke over Kolkata Airport, the terminal buzzed with an undercurrent of excitement and urgency, yet for us, it felt as though time had slowed. Each moment lingered as we gripped our boarding passes and passports, our hearts pounding with anticipation. This wasn't just a simple holiday; it was the first chapter of our life's grand journey together—our honeymoon, a celebration of love, promises, and new beginnings. For the first time as a married couple, we were venturing beyond familiar borders, setting off on an international adventure that we had dreamt about for years. It felt surreal, as if the very air around us was charged with our hopes and excitement.

As our plane lifted off, I looked at Krittika, her eyes mirroring my own awe and joy. We shared a silent smile, a mutual acknowledgment of this long-awaited moment. The past months had been a whirlwind of wedding preparations and celebrations, but now it was just the two of us, embracing a dream we had nurtured for so long. Our love felt amplified in that fleeting moment of ascent, as we watched the ground fade beneath us, replaced by a seemingly endless sky. Our journey had begun.

During our layover in Bangkok, we strolled hand-in-hand through the bustling terminal, soaking in the vibrant mix of people from different cultures, languages, and backgrounds. The lively sounds around us felt like music—snippets of laughter, foreign words, and announcements in languages we couldn't understand but found fascinating. The scents of exotic foods from the food stalls teased our senses, and the sheer diversity of experiences within that one airport hinted at the world waiting to be discovered. Every step brought a new sight, sound, or aroma, intensifying our anticipation for what lay ahead. Though we were still hours from our final destination, our honeymoon felt well underway.

Finally, after hours of travel, layovers, and impatient clock-watching, we touched down in Denpasar, Bali. As we exited the plane, the warmth of the tropical air greeted us, a stark contrast to the cold, recycled air of the aircraft cabin. It was early evening, and the Balinese sun hung low in the sky, casting a golden light that softened the surrounding landscape. In the distance, lush green hills rolled gently, framing the horizon, while clusters of tall palm trees swayed gracefully in the breeze, welcoming us to this paradise.

We strolled through the airport's corridors, admiring the beautiful architecture that seemed to embody Bali's unique spirit. The walls were adorned with intricate stone carvings and vibrant flower arrangements, offering a taste of the island's culture and heritage. Each carved statue we passed seemed to tell its own story, beckoning us to explore and uncover the mysteries hidden within this new world. We felt as though we were walking through a living museum, with each artifact a piece of the larger, captivating puzzle that was Bali.

As we walked through the bustling arrival area, the hum of conversations and the soft whir of luggage carts seemed to fade into the background. Amidst the sea of travellers, our eyes landed on a man standing just beyond the gates, holding a simple sign with our names written clearly in bold letters. He was dressed in a traditional sarong, the deep colors of his attire blending harmoniously with the vibrant energy of the airport. His presence stood out, exuding a sense of calm and warmth that immediately put us at ease.

As we approached him, his face broke into a wide, genuine smile, and he gave us a slight bow, a gesture of respect that felt both gracious and sincere. His eyes twinkled with friendliness, and the moment our gaze met, we felt a deep sense of welcome, as if we had arrived somewhere special—somewhere that already felt like home.

"Welcome to Bali!" he said, his voice soft but confident, carrying a lilting, melodic accent that danced in the air like the gentle rhythm of traditional Balinese music. The way he spoke felt like a gentle invitation to embrace the island's warmth and culture. "Is this your first time here?" he asked, his tone carrying the same warmth as his smile, making us feel as though we were being welcomed into the heart of Bali itself.

There was something enchanting about the way he spoke, as though each word was carefully chosen to make us feel like honoured guests. His calm demeanor and the genuine interest in our experience made the chaotic buzz of the airport fade into the background, replaced by a deep sense of serenity. It was as though

Bali itself had greeted us through him, its spirit already wrapping us in a sense of peace and anticipation for the adventures that lay ahead.

"Yes, and it's our honeymoon," Krittika replied, her voice brimming with excitement and joy.

"Oh! Congratulations!" he exclaimed, clapping his hands together in a gesture of celebration. "Bali is the perfect place for love and new beginnings. You will find happiness here." His words, spoken with an almost musical cadence, felt like a blessing, a promise from Bali itself.

During our ride to the car rental agency, our driver shared stories about his life in Bali, offering glimpses into the culture and recommending places we should explore. "You must visit the temples," he said, catching our eyes in the rearview mirror. "They are the soul of Bali. Each one has its own spirit, its own story. And the beaches are more than just beautiful—they have their own personalities. You will see."

His words flowed like a gentle stream, painting vivid images in our minds, each description adding layers of anticipation to our journey. As he spoke of Bali's sacred temples, we could almost feel the quiet reverence of the stone walls, the scent of incense wafting through the air, and the sense of history that seemed to hum from the ancient structures. His voice carried a reverence for each place he described, transforming each temple into more than just a monument—it became a living testament to the island's spiritual heart.

When he spoke of the beaches, his enthusiasm made the very idea of stepping onto those shores feel like an invitation to a secret paradise. The idea of standing at the edge of the turquoise waters, watching the waves crash against sun-warmed sand, made our excitement surge. His descriptions of hidden coves, sparkling shores, and the salty breeze whispered of adventure and discovery. It felt as though he was not just giving directions but sharing a treasure map to a place filled with wonder.

Every word he spoke seemed to open up new doors of possibility, each destination becoming more than just a location—it became a piece of magic, a place where nature and culture blended in perfect harmony. The excitement in his voice was contagious, pulling us deeper into the idea of Bali not just as a place to visit, but as a place to experience deeply, to feel its soul, to be changed by it.

By the time we arrived at the car rental agency, we felt as though we had already taken our first steps into Bali's heart. We hadn't even left the airport yet, but it already felt like the island had woven itself into our very being. We were filled with a quiet excitement, a knowing that the journey ahead would be unlike anything we had experienced before. It was as if we were already part of Bali's rhythm, ready to embrace whatever it had in store for us.

We picked up the keys to our rental car, a modest white Toyota Agya, perfect for navigating Bali's narrow, winding roads. As I took the driver's seat, a blend of thrill and apprehension washed over me. Driving in a foreign country, especially one so lively and unpredictable, was both exhilarating and intimidating. Krittika's reassuring smile eased my nerves, grounding me in the moment. With a deep breath, I turned on the ignition, and we were on our way to Kuta, Bali's famous beach town, known for its vibrant atmosphere and stunning sunsets.

Our drive to Kuta was an experience unto itself. The streets were lined with charming shops displaying colourful sarongs, intricate jewellery, and handmade crafts. Outside each business, small offerings—woven baskets filled with flowers, rice, and incense—sat humbly on the ground, filling the air with a fragrant blend of floral and sandalwood scents. These offerings, known as "canang sari," were a reminder of the island's deep spirituality and its seamless integration into daily life. Seeing these small acts of devotion scattered across the bustling streets made me feel both humbled and honoured to be here, a guest in a land so rich in tradition.

As we arrived in Kuta, we parked the car and decided to explore the lively area on foot. The streets thrummed with energy; locals and tourists alike moved with a shared sense of joy and excitement. A group of teenagers whizzed by on scooters, laughing and shouting, while a street vendor called out, "Satay! Fresh satay!" The enticing aroma of grilled meat and spices wafted through the air, tempting us to stop and indulge. We couldn't resist and soon found ourselves savouring skewers of juicy, perfectly seasoned satay—a flavour that felt like a taste of Bali's heart.

Just as we reached Kuta Beach, the sky began its daily transformation, painted with hues of orange, pink, and gold. The soft, golden sands stretched out before us, meeting the calm waves that rolled onto the shore in gentle, rhythmic whispers. We stood in awe as the sun slowly dipped below the horizon, casting its warm light across the water. The scene felt almost surreal, like a perfect painting brought to life, crafted just for us in this intimate moment.

As we wandered along the shore, hand in hand, we noticed a small gathering of people, each of them silently watching the sunset with reverence. Drawn by curiosity, we joined the group, catching snippets of conversations in languages we recognized and others we did not. A young woman turned to us and smiled warmly. "Isn't it beautiful?" she asked, her accent American.

"It's breathtaking," I replied, feeling an overwhelming sense of awe and gratitude.

She nodded, her gaze drifting back to the horizon. "I've traveled a lot, but there's something about Bali. It has a peace, a balance that I haven't felt anywhere else. This island… it's special."

Krittika and I shared a knowing glance, silently agreeing. Bali's magic was not just in its beauty but in the harmony, it fostered—a quiet connection between the land, the sea, and the people who called it home. We spent some time-sharing stories with the small group, exchanging travel tips and laughter before we eventually parted ways, the beach gradually emptying as night settled in.

Returning to our car, exhaustion began to settle in, though our spirits remained high. Krittika placed her hand over mine as I gripped the steering wheel, and in that simple gesture, I felt a profound sense of peace and unity. This journey was not just about exploring Bali; it was about exploring life together, discovering each other anew in this new setting.

As we drove back to our hotel, the streets of Bali seemed to slow down in harmony with the softening light of the late afternoon. The usual hum of the day had faded into a serene quietness, the air cooling with the approaching evening. The contrast between the lively energy of the day and this peaceful twilight hour was striking. We passed through neighborhoods where the vibrant greens of the rice fields met the golden glow of the setting sun, and the simplicity of it all felt profound.

Along the roadside, locals were carefully arranging their offerings—small plates of delicate flowers, rice, and incense—arranged with quiet reverence. The scent of burning incense began to mingle with the air, adding to the atmosphere of calm. Lanterns in various shapes and sizes were being lit with meticulous care, their flames flickering softly against the shadows. Each little gesture felt like a prayer, a piece of daily life that honored both tradition and the divine. It wasn't just ritual; it was a rhythm, a quiet pulse that reverberated through the streets, the island, and even through us.

I couldn't shake the feeling that Bali had already accepted us, that we had been quietly welcomed into its embrace. The island, in its simplicity, felt like a living entity, one that spoke not through grand gestures, but through small moments of grace. The beauty was in the details—those humble offerings, the warm glow of lanterns, the smiles exchanged between strangers—that somehow made it feel like the island had always known we would be here.

It was in the stillness of these moments that I felt a deep connection, a sense that Bali was not just a destination, but a living, breathing presence that invited us to be a part of its story. Every sight, every interaction, felt like an invitation to immerse ourselves more fully, to let go of our expectations, and to simply embrace each moment with an open heart. The island's magic wasn't just in its breathtaking landscapes or spiritual landmarks—it was in the way it made us feel welcome, like we were stepping into a story that had been unfolding long before our arrival. The warmth of Bali had already begun to seep into us, and we couldn't wait to see where this journey would take us next.

Later that night, as we lay in bed, the air was cool and filled with the faint, soothing rhythm of the waves crashing in the distance. The sound, almost like a lullaby, gently echoed through the room, lulling us into a tranquil slumber. Each wave seemed to whisper its own story, a timeless reminder of the vast ocean beyond our window, endlessly stretching out into the unknown. In those moments, the world outside felt both immense and intimate, a reminder of the beauty that lay waiting for us to discover.

The room was dim, with only the soft glow of moonlight filtering through the curtains, casting delicate shadows across the floor. The stillness around us was comforting, almost sacred, as if the entire island was holding its breath along with us, letting the night unfold at its own pace. I could feel Krittika's hand resting gently in mine, the warmth of her touch grounding me, making everything feel right. In that quiet moment, I felt an overwhelming sense of peace, a quiet contentment that settled deep in my chest.

A flood of gratitude washed over me. We had come to this island seeking adventure, yes, but we had found so much more—love, connection, and a deeper understanding of the world and each other. Our journey together, which had begun with a sense of curiosity, had already woven its way into something far more meaningful. I realized that this wasn't just a vacation; it was the start of a chapter in our lives that we would look back on forever. Bali had already begun to shape our hearts and minds, and I knew that it would stay with us long after we left.

As the night deepened, I closed my eyes, filled with gratitude for every step of this journey—every shared laugh, every breathtaking view, every quiet moment between us. Tomorrow, we would wake to a new day, with the first light of Bali touching its shores, and we would be ready to dive into the adventure ahead. We didn't know where the next moment would take us, but with each new day, we would embrace it together, knowing that every step we took in this beautiful place would become a treasured part of our story.

Chapter 2: Sacred Morning at Tanah Lot

March 7, 2024

The alarm buzzed sharply at 4:00 a.m., piercing through the heavy silence of the early morning and jolting us awake in the cozy darkness of our hotel room. For a moment, we lay there, cocooned in the warmth of sleep, wrapped in the lingering comfort of the night. The early hour felt surreal; our minds struggled to shake off the remnants of dreams, leaving us briefly uncertain if we were still dreaming or if this was indeed the start of our new adventure. But as the haze of sleep began to clear, a rush of excitement took its place, reminding us exactly why we were up before dawn. Today, we would experience one of Bali's most revered sights: the sunrise over Tanah Lot Temple.

Eager to begin the day, we slipped out of bed, careful not to disturb the quiet. Dressing quickly, we layered up against the morning chill that was unfamiliar in tropical Bali. By 4:30, we were out the door. Outside, our little Toyota Agya waited, its white frame barely visible in the soft predawn light. The engine purred to life, and as we eased onto the road, it felt like the island was still asleep, holding its breath in anticipation of the day.

The streets of Bali, usually alive with people and the vibrant sounds of scooters zipping by, were now hushed and empty, illuminated only by a few scattered streetlights. The world outside was dark and serene, like a secret waiting to be unveiled with the first rays of sunlight. In this early hour, Bali's beauty felt intimate, almost as if it was sharing a private moment with us, hidden beneath the shroud of night.

As we drove, the landscape began to transform. Towering trees lined the roadside, their tall shadows swaying gently as a cool breeze swept through their branches. Small shrines appeared at intervals along the road, their shapes barely discernible in the dim light. These shrines, we knew, were places of devotion, where locals would leave daily offerings to honor the spirits of the land and sea. Occasionally, we would pass by small houses, the faint glow of lights from within suggesting that someone was already awake, perhaps preparing for a day of fishing, farming, or market selling. Despite the early hour, the presence of these lights felt reassuring, a reminder of the quiet but steady rhythm of life in Bali.

After an hour of winding through narrow roads and listening to the gentle hum of the engine, we finally arrived at Tanah Lot. The sky above was still dark, though it had begun to soften, a subtle shift from black to deep purple and then to hints of pink and blue. The cool morning air carried the salty scent of the nearby sea, refreshing and invigorating as we stepped out of the car. With a sense of anticipation, we made our way along the sandy path that led to the temple. Our footsteps crunched softly against the earth, blending with the rhythmic sound of waves crashing against the rocks.

As we drew nearer, the silhouette of Tanah Lot began to materialize against the dusky sky, its form emerging slowly from the shadows. The temple seemed to float above the ocean, perched elegantly atop a dramatic rock formation that rose from the sea like a guardian of ancient times. Bathed in the fading glow of the evening light, it had an almost surreal quality—something out of a dream or a painting. It stood not just as a structure, but as a symbol of Bali's spiritual heart, an island that effortlessly fused nature and reverence into one.

The sight took our breath away. The temple, with its intricate carvings and tiered roof, exuded an air of quiet majesty, while the surrounding waters added an element of humility, as if Tanah Lot was simply another part of the natural world, bound together with the land and sea. The waves crashed violently against the base of the rock, sending up sprays of white foam that glistened in the golden light. Each splash felt like an offering, a tribute from the ocean itself to the sacred grounds that had stood there for centuries. The rhythmic sound of the waves, accompanied by the scent of saltwater, seemed to envelop us, transporting us into a different realm where time stood still, and the world was at peace.

The energy of the place was palpable, as if the very air around us held a sacred charge. It was hard to describe, but there was an undeniable sense of reverence in the atmosphere, one that transcended words. We stood there for a long moment, simply taking it all in—the awe-inspiring view, the crash of the ocean, and the tranquil spirituality of Tanah Lot. In that brief, perfect instant, it felt as though we were standing on the edge of the world, connected to something much larger than ourselves. Nature and spirituality were intertwined, and we were merely guests in this timeless, sacred space.

In that moment, Bali's spirit seemed to speak directly to us, as if the island itself was inviting us to pause, reflect, and feel the profound connection between humanity and the natural world. It wasn't just the physical beauty of Tanah Lot that left us speechless, but the way it seemed to embody the heart of Bali—its devotion, its harmony with nature, and its eternal reverence for the divine. We stood in quiet admiration, knowing that this was one of those rare moments in life where you felt truly connected to something greater than yourself.

We took out our camera, a mix of excitement and nervousness bubbling up as we prepared to record our first vlog for our YouTube Channel named "Teering Beering". Holding the camera up, I smiled at Krittika, who stood beside me, her face softly illuminated by the faint morning light. "Welcome to Bali!" I said, my voice barely above a whisper, as though speaking too loudly might disturb the tranquillity of the scene. Krittika introduced us to our viewers, her excitement mirrored in her warm smile. Sharing this moment felt special, as if we weren't just documenting a trip but inviting others into a piece of our lives, allowing them to experience this magic alongside us.

Only a handful of people were there, scattered across the temple grounds, each drawn to this sacred place by the promise of the rising sun. The near solitude made the experience even more profound. The silence was profound, interrupted only by the steady rhythm of the waves and the occasional murmur of another early riser, just as awestruck by the scene.

"Good morning!" a warm voice greeted us softly from beside. We turned to see an older man, perhaps in his sixties, with a gentle smile and wise eyes. Dressed in a traditional Balinese sarong and a woven basket filled with offerings, he exuded an aura of peace and reverence.

"Good morning," I replied, returning his smile.

"You are here early, very good," he said in a lilting, musical accent. "The gods bless those who come before the crowds. Tanah Lot is at its most beautiful when it is still, before the sun fully rises."

"We can feel it," Krittika replied, her voice filled with awe. "There's something magical here."

The man nodded knowingly. "Yes, this is a holy place. In Bali, we believe Tanah Lot is protected by sea snakes, spirits of the ocean. They guard the temple from harm." He gestured toward the rocks below, where shadows clung to the edges. "You may not see them, but they are here."

We peered over the edge, squinting to catch a glimpse of these legendary guardians, though we couldn't see anything. Yet the sense of mystery only deepened our admiration for the temple, adding a layer of enchantment to the experience. The temple felt alive, as if it carried secrets within its walls, holding the wisdom of generations past.

The man carefully lifted a small offering from his basket—a creation of woven palm leaves, fresh flowers, and a sprinkle of rice. "In Bali, we make offerings like this every day," he explained. "For us, life is a balance of energies. We give thanks, ask for blessings, and make peace with the spirits of the land and sea."

With a gentle smile, he handed us each an offering, inviting us to place them at the temple's entrance. Following his lead, we knelt down, feeling the cool earth beneath us, and gently placed our offerings by the entrance. It was a simple gesture but one that felt deeply significant, a way to connect with the spirituality that permeated Bali's landscapes and way of life.

"Thank you," I said, feeling a swell of gratitude for this small but meaningful act. In that moment, the temple, the waves, and even the man beside us felt like parts of a single, harmonious whole, connected by an invisible thread.

As we rose, the sky began to lighten, casting a warm, golden glow over Tanah Lot. The waves turned from dark blue to shimmering shades of silver and gold, catching the first hints of sunlight. We watched in silence as the temple seemed to awaken with the dawn, its silhouette glowing softly, framed by the colours of morning.

Just then, another couple approached, stopping beside us with wide smiles. They introduced themselves as Emma and Chris, travellers from Sydney. They had been exploring Southeast Asia for weeks, they told us, captivated by new cultures and landscapes.

"Isn't this place incredible?" Emma asked, her Australian accent bright with excitement. "It's like a scene from a dream."

We nodded, sharing a smile of understanding. "It's our first time in Bali, and I don't think we could have imagined anything like this," I replied.

Chris looked over at the temple, his eyes reflecting the light of the rising sun. "We were in Thailand last week, but there's something about Bali that just… speaks to you. It's more than just the scenery."

I couldn't agree more. "It's like every part of the island has a story, a soul," I said, trying to capture the feeling we had felt since our arrival.

We stood together, strangers brought together by a shared sense of wonder, each of us connected by our appreciation for the beauty around us. The silence that followed felt profound, each of us lost in our own reflections, grateful to witness this moment.

As the sun peeked over the horizon, its first rays illuminated the temple in a soft, golden light. Tanah Lot seemed to shimmer under the dawn's blessing, the waves turning pink and orange as they caught the sunlight. The entire scene felt alive, as if the spirits of the ocean and the land were joining in a quiet celebration of the new day.

More visitors began to arrive, their voices gently breaking the silence. Though the stillness was fading, the temple remained as breathtaking as ever. We took one last, lingering look, trying to imprint every detail in our minds before turning back to the path.

The drive back was quiet, both of us wrapped in our thoughts, carrying the peace of Tanah Lot with us like a warm, lingering embrace. There was a sense of calm that neither of us wanted to disrupt, a feeling so profound that it seemed to settle deeply into our bones. As the car hummed along the winding roads, surrounded by the gentle waking sounds of the island, I glanced over at Krittika, noticing how the early sunlight cast a soft glow on her face. Her eyes were distant, reflecting the same quiet awe I felt, as if we had both just touched something sacred. We exchanged a small smile, acknowledging without words the impact of the experience we had shared.

In those quiet moments, I realized that we had witnessed more than just the beauty of a sunrise; we had become a part of something timeless and ancient, a story woven into the fabric of Bali itself. We had stood in the presence of a powerful harmony that transcended the everyday and the familiar. It was more than a scenic view; it was a living connection to the essence of the island, an energy that felt as if it had been preserved across centuries and that now welcomed us with open arms. A sunrise like that had an essence of its own, something that couldn't be captured fully in words or even in the recording on our camera. It was an experience of feeling small yet profoundly connected to a vast world beyond our understanding.

As the landscape continued to pass by, dotted with small shrines and sleepy villages still waking up to the day, I wondered how many others had felt this same sense of awe at Tanah Lot and how many lives that temple had touched. The temple stood resolute against the ocean's waves, unmoved by the passing of time, a silent witness to the lives, joys, and sorrows of generations. It was humbling to think that we had joined the ranks of so many who had come before us, drawn by the same magnetic beauty.

Returning from such a powerful place brought a bittersweet feeling, a sense of longing even as we were only just beginning our time on the island. There was something indescribable about those early hours at Tanah Lot—a quiet, rare gift, as if the universe had handed us a precious moment to hold close. In that simple drive back, I felt a peaceful kind of gratitude, one that softened any concerns or anxieties about the days ahead. Krittika reached over and gently squeezed my hand, grounding us both in that beautiful, fleeting reality, a moment that would stay etched in our memories for years to come.

As the first morning rays began to brighten the roads and fields, I thought about what other wonders Bali might reveal to us. The island felt alive with secrets, as if it held a story in every mountain, forest, and temple. What else might we discover? What other encounters with nature, spirit, and history awaited us? Bali seemed to offer endless possibilities, each hidden corner ready to share something magical and profound with those willing to explore with an open heart.

Looking over at Krittika, I could sense she was feeling the same way—her gaze held a hint of anticipation, a shared understanding that we were only scratching the surface of all the island had to offer. That morning at Tanah Lot was just the beginning of a journey, a prologue to the adventure that lay ahead, filled with beauty, wonder, and stories waiting to be told. Bali had revealed a piece of its heart to us, but we knew it was only the first chapter in a much larger story, one we would uncover day by day, step by step, memory by memory.

Chapter 3: Uluwatu's Majesty and the Hidden Gem of Suluban

March 7, 2024

After the soulful start to our day at Tanah Lot, we set off for our next destination, Uluwatu Temple, with the excitement of new experiences buzzing between us. The drive was nothing short of enchanting, taking us through winding roads bordered by tall, swaying coconut palms. As we wove in and out of Bali's green cliffs, the glint of the blue ocean would occasionally peek through the trees, teasing us with glimpses of the turquoise expanse that lay ahead. Our little Toyota Agya was more than just a vehicle that day; it felt like a carriage on a pilgrimage, carrying us through the mystical landscapes of Bali toward another sacred place.

Uluwatu was famous for its breathtaking clifftop views and for being one of Bali's directional temples, standing guard over the island from its lofty perch high above the sea. In Balinese Hinduism, these directional temples are believed to protect the island from evil spirits, and each one is considered a gateway into the spiritual heart of Bali. Knowing that we were about to visit such a revered location heightened our anticipation, and we found ourselves speaking in hushed tones, as if the sacred energy surrounding Uluwatu could already be felt on the breeze.

As we drew closer, the landscape transformed. Gentle hills gave way to steep cliffs, each one more dramatic than the last, plunging straight down to the ocean below. The air was thick with the scent of salt and wildflowers, carried by the warm breeze that rolled in from the sea. Uluwatu Temple came into view like a vision, perched proudly on the edge of a towering cliff, its ancient stone walls weathered yet resilient. It was a scene that belonged in a storybook—a grand structure crowned with greenery, appearing almost as if it were growing out of the earth itself, a natural extension of the island.

Standing at the edge of Uluwatu Temple, we found ourselves completely captivated by the sheer, untamed beauty that stretched out before us. The landscape was almost surreal, like a scene painted by the most imaginative of artists. The ocean, vast and seemingly endless, rolled toward the cliffs in waves that gleamed under the sunlight, each crest catching the light and then crashing against the rocks below with a thunderous power. There was something profoundly humbling about being so close to nature's raw strength and elegance all at once.

We felt the pull of the horizon, where the turquoise water met the sky in a seamless blend of blues, broken only by the gentle sweep of clouds drifting lazily. Every gust of wind carried the scent of salt and blooming wildflowers, adding to the sensory experience that was more immersive than anything we'd felt before. The cliffs themselves were like ancient guardians, rising steeply from the ocean, each one covered in a layer of lush greenery that danced in the breeze, seeming to sway to some silent rhythm only nature could hear.

As we panned our camera to capture the view, we found ourselves pausing every few moments, drawn in by the panoramic grandeur. It was a scene so majestic that even our words fell short, as if any attempt to describe it would somehow diminish the experience. There was a tranquil energy in the air, a feeling that we had stumbled upon a place where time held its breath—a sacred meeting point of land, sea, and sky that seemed to transcend anything we could fully comprehend.

In that moment, standing on the cliff's edge with the world stretching endlessly before us, we felt an undeniable connection to something much larger than ourselves. Uluwatu Temple was not just a place to see, but a place to feel, to become a part of, if only for a moment. It was a view that left us mesmerized, rooted in awe, and eternally grateful for the chance to witness such unspoiled beauty.

At the temple entrance, we were greeted by temple staff who offered us traditional sarongs to wrap around our waists. The sarongs, with their bold colours and intricate patterns, were both practical and symbolic, serving as a reminder of the respect we owed to the temple and the spirituality it embodied. The ritual of wrapping ourselves in the sarongs felt grounding, a way of aligning ourselves with the temple's sacredness and becoming, however briefly, a part of its world.

As we began filming, we moved carefully, conscious of the quiet reverence permeating the temple grounds. The atmosphere was both solemn and inviting, and although there were other visitors around us, an unspoken understanding seemed to prevail, as if everyone had come with a shared sense of awe. We lowered our voices as we narrated to the camera, pausing frequently to capture the view and just take in the sheer beauty of the place.

From the cliff's edge, the ocean stretched endlessly, the waves rolling and crashing in an almost musical rhythm against the rocks far below. The water was a brilliant, vivid blue, deepening as it neared the horizon, and each wave seemed to carry with it an energy that was at once powerful and peaceful. The scene was breathtaking, and although we tried to capture it on video, we both knew that no lens could fully convey the experience of standing there, suspended between sky and sea.

A Balinese man noticed our camera and approached us with a friendly smile. Dressed in a traditional white shirt and sarong, he introduced himself with a gentle wave and a warm, inviting gaze. "You are vlogging, yes?" he asked, nodding toward our camera.

We smiled back, nodding. "Yes, we're new to Bali," I replied. "It's so incredible here. We're trying to capture as much as we can."

The man nodded thoughtfully, his eyes twinkling. "Bali is a place of spirits, of energy," he said. "Uluwatu is one of the six main temples, dedicated to protecting Bali from the sea. You will see more and more if you look with an open heart."

He gestured toward the temple, his voice softening with reverence as he spoke of its significance. "Uluwatu Temple is more than just a sacred site," he began. "It is one of Bali's most important spiritual pillars, guarding the island from negative influences and protecting the balance between nature and the divine." He looked out toward the endless ocean, his eyes tracing the horizon, as if drawing strength from the very view. "It is a temple of great power—standing on these cliffs, it connects the earth with the sea and the sky."

His tone was gentle but filled with a deep respect, as if the temple itself were alive with spirit. "Bali's temples are not just places of worship, but guardians of the island's soul. Uluwatu, in particular, is believed to ward off evil spirits, watching over the land with its powerful energy," he continued. "The Balinese believe that the temple's position, high above the crashing waves, acts as a shield, keeping the island safe from harm."

He paused, letting the words sink in, before adding with a knowing smile, "But Uluwatu also teaches us something important: to respect the forces of nature—the sea, the wind, the sky—and they, in return, will show us their beauty. The temple is a reminder to live in harmony with the world around us."

Looking back at the temple as the evening sun painted the sky with shades of orange and purple, he spoke once more. "The spirits of the temple are not distant or abstract. They are here, in the wind that whispers through the cliffs, in the sound of the waves crashing below. They are part of the island, and we are part of them. Respect the sea, respect the spirits, and you will understand the true beauty of Bali."

His words resonated with us deeply, and as we stood there, gazing at Uluwatu Temple with its ancient stone walls and breathtaking view, we felt a connection to something greater. The temple was not just a place of worship—it was a living presence that stood as a testament to Bali's deep spiritual heritage. Through his words, we understood that Bali's beauty was not just in its landscapes, but in the respect and reverence for the natural world that its people held so dear.

As he spoke, a group of monkeys darted past, their lively chatter breaking the serene silence. These macaques were known as the temple's unofficial residents, and they had earned quite a reputation for their curiosity—and their tendency to snatch anything they could get their paws on. We watched, laughing with other visitors as the monkeys eyed sunglasses and hats with mischief in their eyes, occasionally darting in for a quick "borrow." They added a light-hearted energy to the experience, a reminder that even in places of deep spirituality, life and playfulness found their way.

Once we'd explored the temple grounds, we made our way to the cliff's edge to film the sweeping views of the ocean below. Standing there, on the very edge of Bali, we felt a profound sense of peace, as if the waves crashing far below were carrying away our cares, replacing them with something far greater than ourselves. The ocean stretched on forever, and we were simply two small figures on its shore, witnesses to its vast, timeless beauty.

With our hearts brimming with gratitude and awe, and our camera filled with footage capturing the unforgettable beauty of Uluwatu, we reluctantly left the temple's sacred grounds. The experience had left us feeling both humbled by the raw, powerful beauty of nature and invigorated by the spiritual energy that seemed to pulse through the very air around us. The sight of the vast ocean crashing against the cliffs, coupled with the peaceful aura of the temple, had awakened something inside of us—a deeper appreciation for the natural world and the profound sense of connection that can be found when one truly stops to witness it. As we made our way back to our car, the sense of serenity still lingered, yet there was a growing sense of excitement as we turned our attention to what lay ahead.

The road to Suluban Beach stretched out before us, winding through Bali's lush, vibrant landscape. As we drove, we couldn't help but feel that this was only the beginning of our journey—that Bali, with all its mystery and allure, still had much more to reveal. Each twist of the road seemed to hold the promise of a new discovery, and we eagerly anticipated the hidden treasures that lay ahead. The island's natural beauty, its spiritual energy, and the people we encountered along the way had already left an indelible mark on us. Yet we sensed that there were still countless more stories to unfold, each one more captivating than the last. With the sun now higher in the sky and our spirits soaring, we looked forward to immersing ourselves in the next chapter of our Bali adventure, knowing that whatever we encountered, it would be yet another piece of this island's enchanting puzzle.

Suluban Beach, hidden beneath another cliff just a short drive from Uluwatu, was famed as a surfer's paradise, known for its challenging waves and its secretive, secluded location. The journey to the beach itself was an adventure, as we descended steep stone steps carved into the cliffside, winding our way down through narrow passages. With every step, the sound of the waves grew louder, and the excitement in our hearts quickened.

When we finally emerged onto the beach, we were greeted by a surreal sight: a small, crescent-shaped shoreline nestled between towering cliffs and sea caves. The beach was secluded, shielded from the world above by its rugged cliffs, and the only people here were a handful of surfers and explorers like us. The scene felt like something out of a dream, with the sun casting a soft glow over the turquoise water, illuminating the hidden pools and caves formed by the rock.

We struck up a conversation with one of the surfers, a sun-tanned Australian named Matt. He'd been visiting Bali for years, and his love for the island was obvious. "This place is special," he said, grinning as he gestured to the waves. "Not easy to reach, but that's the magic of it. Keeps the crowds away, you know?"

We nodded, understanding exactly what he meant. Suluban felt like a hidden world, a private sanctuary carved out by nature. The water was crystal clear, and as we set up our camera to film, we couldn't help but marvel at the way Suluban balanced power and serenity.

The waves were fierce and untamed, yet the water lapped gently at the edges of the caves, creating a calm, rhythmic music.

Krittika was wandering along the sun-dappled shoreline of Suluban Beach, her eyes lost in the rhythmic dance of the waves as they crashed against the rocks. I followed closely behind, capturing the beauty of the moment on camera. The beach, tucked away between towering cliffs, was surprisingly quiet, with only the occasional surfer gliding effortlessly across the waves. The air was warm, carrying the scent of saltwater and wildflowers, and the sound of the ocean seemed to synchronize with the pulse of our own quiet excitement. As we meandered further along the beach, a short, blonde woman approached Krittika, her figure framed by the brilliant sunlight. With a friendly smile, she asked in a soft German accent if Krittika would mind taking some photos of her. Krittika, ever the gracious soul, smiled warmly and agreed without hesitation. I watched as Krittika adjusted the camera, capturing different angles of the woman, who posed with a natural grace, her blonde hair catching the light like strands of gold. The woman's energy was easy-going, and she chatted with Krittika between shots, clearly enjoying the experience. After a few minutes, she turned to Krittika, her face lighting up with genuine warmth. "Are you from India?" she asked, her blue eyes sparkling. "You are so beautiful," she added, her compliment soft yet sincere. Krittika, blushing slightly, thanked her in return, her heart-warming at the kindness of this stranger. The exchange was brief but filled with an unspoken connection, a reminder of how travel brings people together, even for a fleeting moment, and how the simple act of a compliment can brighten a day.

As we explored the beach, we waded through shallow pools and wandered into shadowed coves, each one like its own secret world. The cliffs towered above us, their dark, jagged faces softened by the green foliage spilling over their edges. It was as though the earth itself was embracing the beach, offering it as a gift to those willing to make the journey down.

After a few hours of filming, hunger reminded us that it was time for a break. We climbed back up to a small, rustic café we had noticed earlier, perched on the cliffside with a breathtaking view of the beach below. The café was simple, with only a handful of tables and chairs beneath a thatched canopy, but it was perfect. We ordered some local dishes, eager to taste the flavours of Indonesia.

The waiter brought us a plate of 'ayam bakar'—grilled chicken marinated in a blend of spices that filled the air with a mouthwatering aroma. It was served with steamed rice, fresh greens, and sambal, the spicy chili sauce that's a staple in Indonesian cuisine. We savoured every bite, the spices bold and fragrant, warming us from the inside out.

As we ate, the sun began to dip lower in the sky, casting a golden glow over Suluban Beach. The surfers were still out, riding the waves with ease and grace, and we watched them with admiration, marvelling at their skill and the harmony they seemed to have with the ocean.

As the sun began to set, painting the sky with hues of pink and orange, we took one last, lingering look at Suluban Beach, trying to imprint every detail in our memories. The waves glistened with the colours of the sunset, each crest catching the light like liquid fire. It was a sight we would carry with us long after we left.

With our legs tired from the climb and our spirits rejuvenated, we made our way back to the car, feeling deeply connected to the island and its wonders. The drive back was peaceful, with the stars beginning to emerge in the sky above. Bali had already shown us so much, yet we knew it had only just begun to reveal itself to us. The island's secrets, its stories, and its spirit lay before us, waiting to be discovered, and we were eager to embrace every moment.

As the day came to a close, we found ourselves seated in a charming open-air café in Kuta, the sky above us a canvas of warm hues from the setting sun. The café, nestled on a quiet corner, was the perfect spot to unwind after a day filled with adventure. The cool evening breeze rustled the leaves of nearby trees, and the sound of gentle conversations and clinking glasses blended with the distant hum of the ocean waves. We sipped on cold drinks, savouring the flavours of fresh tropical fruit and local delicacies, as the last golden rays of sunlight dipped below the horizon. With the stars beginning to twinkle above us, there was a quiet sense of anticipation in the air. We shared a smile, knowing that the day had been incredible, yet we couldn't shake the feeling that Bali still had so much more to reveal. Tomorrow, we whispered to each other, holding onto the excitement of the unknown. There was something magical about the island that promised new surprises at every turn, and as the night settled in, we couldn't help but feel that the next day would be just as extraordinary—*if not more*.

Chapter 4: Gates of Paradise and the Road to Hidden Beauty

March 8, 2024

Once again, we rose with the sun, eager for the promise of a new day in Bali. At 4:30 a.m., we quietly slipped out of our cozy room, the island still wrapped in the peaceful embrace of night. The cool air kissed our skin as we hopped on the scooter, the roads ahead empty and quiet, save for the soft hum of the engine and the faint rustle of leaves in the breeze. The only light came from the faint glow of our headlights and the dim, pre-dawn hues that stretched across the sky. There was something magical about the early morning—like the world was still waking up, and we had a brief moment to experience it in its most serene state.

The excitement was palpable as we drove through the stillness, the silence broken only by the occasional chirp of crickets and the distant call of a bird beginning its day. Our destination was the Handara Gate, an iconic landmark that had captured our imaginations since we first saw it in photos. Its towering stone arches, flanked by lush greenery and dramatic mountain backdrops, had promised an experience of awe, and now, we were on our way to see it with our own eyes.

The landscape around us slowly began to shift as the sky lightened, revealing Bali's stunning terrain—rolling hills, dense forests, and distant peaks that were just beginning to be bathed in the soft pinks and oranges of the early morning light. The sense of anticipation grew with each turn of the road, the journey feeling almost like a sacred pilgrimage. We could sense the specialness of the moment, like we were about to enter a space where the natural world and Bali's spiritual essence converged.

As we approached the gate, we could make out its imposing silhouette through the mist that hung in the air, the mountains rising behind it like ancient guardians. The gate itself, with its ornate stone carvings, stood tall and proud against the backdrop of lush green fields. It looked every bit as stunning as the photographs had promised—and more. This wasn't just a photo opportunity, but a living, breathing testament to the island's beauty and its cultural significance.

We parked the scooter and walked toward the gate, the air fresh and crisp, carrying the scent of earth and greenery. The feeling of being there, standing before this majestic structure, was surreal. The towering gate seemed to draw us in, inviting us to step through and explore what lay beyond. The landscape stretched out before us, a breathtaking panorama of misty mountains and vibrant, untouched nature. It felt as though we had stepped into another world, where time moved slower and the beauty around us was something sacred to be savoured.

With the sun finally beginning to rise, casting a golden light over the landscape, we stood there in awe, taking in every detail—both the grandeur of the gate and the quiet beauty of the surrounding nature.

In that moment, Bali felt timeless, as if we were witnessing the island's soul laid bare. This was more than just a famous landmark; it was a reminder of Bali's deep connection to its natural and spiritual world. The excitement of the morning had been more than met—it had exceeded every expectation, and we were ready to experience more.

As we drove, the beauty of Bali's countryside unfolded in a series of magical scenes. We passed through small, peaceful villages, where clusters of wooden homes stood nestled among rice fields that stretched out in a lush, green sea, blanketed by the soft mist of early morning. Farmers were just beginning their day, bent over in the fields, their faces lined with the wisdom of the land. Some gave us friendly nods or brief waves, a quiet acknowledgment of our shared moment on this island, even as strangers.

At one point, we paused to admire a particularly breathtaking rice terrace, where an older Balinese woman with a woven basket of fresh vegetables on her hip greeted us with a gentle smile. "Selamat pagi!" she called, her voice hearty and full of warmth.

"Selamat pagi!" we replied, our hesitant Bahasa drawing a kind laugh from her. She pointed to Krittika with a gleam in her eye, saying something we couldn't quite understand, but which ended with a thumbs-up, clearly appreciating her outfit and enthusiasm. Krittika laughed, and we waved goodbye, our spirits uplifted by this brief connection.

The road became increasingly winding and narrow as we journeyed further into Bali's mountains, and each turn revealed a fresh glimpse of the island's dramatic landscape. After nearly an hour, we arrived at Handara Gate, where we were the first visitors of the day. The quietness of the place heightened its mystique—the massive stone gate, framed by tall mountains and shrouded in soft morning mist, seemed to hold a spirit of its own. We felt as though we were crossing a threshold, not just into a new place, but into another time, another world.

As we stood before the gate, I fiddled with our camera, trying to capture the quiet majesty of the scene. Suddenly, a young Balinese man in his twenties approached us with a warm smile. Dressed in a traditional sarong, he seemed to exude an air of tranquillity that matched the atmosphere of Handara Gate.

"Need help with the photos?" he asked, his English lilting with a friendly accent.

"Yes, that would be amazing!" I replied, grateful for his offer.

He took the camera with practiced ease, positioning us and suggesting angles we'd never have considered. "Stand here, yes, closer together… very nice," he said with a genuine enthusiasm that made us laugh. He had a keen eye for details, adjusting the camera settings to make the mist around the gate appear almost magical. The morning light created a surreal effect, making the gate appear even more imposing and majestic.

As he continued to take photos, he shared stories of Bali with us, mentioning that he was from a nearby village and had grown up helping tourists capture memories at spots like Handara Gate. "I've been here maybe a thousand times," he chuckled, "but every time, it looks different."

"Do you still find it beautiful after seeing it so much?" Krittika asked, her curiosity piqued.

"Oh yes," he replied, looking at the gate as if seeing it anew. "In Bali, we believe that places like this have a spirit, an energy that changes with each day. Today, it feels very peaceful."

Once we had more photos than we could count, we thanked him sincerely, and he waved us off, calling, "Enjoy Bali, my friends!" His words echoed as we left, adding a touch of warmth to our already glowing spirits.

After leaving Handara Gate with a warm farewell, we set out for our next destination: the enchanting Ulun Danu Beratan Temple. As we drove, the anticipation grew, and the scenic route did not disappoint. Bali continued to surprise us at every turn, the landscape shifting from dense forest to rolling green hills until finally, we reached the edge of Lake Beratan, where the famous temple awaited.

The sight that greeted us was almost surreal, as if we had stepped into a living painting. Ulun Danu Beratan Temple seemed to float effortlessly on the calm waters of Lake Beratan, its pagoda-like structures rising gracefully above the misty lake surface. The reflections of the temple were mirrored perfectly on the glassy water, creating a sense of symmetry and serenity that made it look like a place suspended in time. The stillness of the lake amplified the beauty of the scene, as though the world had paused, holding its breath in awe.

Behind the temple, the misty mountains loomed majestically, their peaks shrouded in a veil of morning fog, adding an ethereal quality to the landscape. The fog hovered like a delicate curtain, partially concealing and revealing the mountains as if they were guardians of this sacred place. The entire scene felt otherworldly—timeless, calm, and deeply spiritual. The temple itself, with its tiered pagodas and intricate carvings, stood in perfect harmony with the natural surroundings, reflecting the island's profound connection between the spiritual and the earthly.

We stood there for a moment, simply absorbing the breathtaking view. It was hard to believe that such beauty existed in the world, let alone that we were fortunate enough to witness it firsthand. The silence around us seemed to magnify the peace of the place, as if the temple, the lake, and the mountains were speaking a language of tranquillity that was understood only by those who were present. It felt like we had stepped directly into a postcard, but even that didn't seem to do the place justice. The moment felt sacred, and in its stillness, we could feel the deep spiritual energy of Bali enveloping us, inviting us to pause, reflect, and be grateful for this incredible experience.

As we approached, we noticed a festive gathering underway. Balinese worshippers, dressed in traditional attire, had gathered at the temple for a special ceremony. The sound of gamelan music filled the air, the soft metallic chimes and rhythmic drums creating a melody that was both soothing and uplifting. The musicians sat in a semi-circle, each focused on their instrument, their fingers moving with skill and precision. It was a captivating display of Bali's cultural vibrancy, and we felt honoured to witness this traditional worship up close.

Krittika and I exchanged awed glances, moved by the serene beauty of the ceremony. "It's like being transported into another world," she murmured, her voice filled with wonder. We stood quietly, allowing the music to wash over us, feeling a sense of reverence for the sacredness of the place.

We continued exploring, taking in the temple's intricate architecture and beautifully sculpted shrines dedicated to various deities. To our surprise, we stumbled upon a statue of Lord Ganesha, the elephant-headed Hindu god who is revered as the remover of obstacles. Seeing this familiar figure in a place so far from home was unexpectedly moving. Krittika smiled and whispered, "It feels like a little piece of Indian culture is here with us." We paused to pay our respects, touched by the connection between Bali's spirituality and our own culture.

As we wandered around the temple grounds, Krittika's camera at the ready, a young Balinese girl caught her attention. The girl, no more than five years old, wore a bright traditional sarong and had flowers adorning her hair, her eyes wide with curiosity. Krittika crouched down, smiling, and asked her mother for permission to take a photo with the girl. The mother nodded, beaming with pride. Krittika gently placed her arm around the girl, who shyly grinned for the camera, her innocent face lighting up the photo. It was a beautiful moment, a small but precious connection that reminded us of the universality of kindness and joy.

The lake itself was another marvel. Lake Beratan stretched out before us, its stillness creating a flawless mirror for the temple and surrounding mountains. The water was so clear it seemed to blend seamlessly with the sky, creating a sense of infinity. We stood by the shore, watching as the gentle ripples moved across the surface, the reflections shifting with each wave. It was a mesmerizing sight, and we felt a profound sense of peace, as if time had slowed just for us to savour the beauty of this place.

As we made our way back to the main pathway, we heard familiar accents behind us. Turning around, we saw a couple who appeared to be from India. They noticed us as well and smiled, introducing themselves as Raktim and Priyanka. It turned out they were also exploring Bali and had been to many of the same spots as us. “Isn’t this temple just magical?” Priyanka exclaimed, her eyes sparkling with the same wonder we felt.

“It’s beyond words,” Krittika replied, nodding enthusiastically. “Every corner of Bali feels like a piece of art.”

We chatted for a while, sharing stories of our travels and exchanging recommendations. Raktim mentioned their plan to visit nearby waterfalls, and we shared some of our own favourite spots, creating a bond over our shared love for exploring. It was refreshing to meet fellow travellers from home, and there was an unspoken understanding between us—the joy of discovering new places, the awe of experiencing different cultures, and the warmth of connecting with strangers.

As we prepared to part ways, Priyanka pulled out her phone for a quick photo together. "Let's remember this beautiful day," she said, and we all smiled for the camera, capturing the moment that now felt like a meeting of friends rather than strangers.

With a sense of gratitude and hearts full of unforgettable memories, we took one last, lingering look at Ulun Danu Beratan Temple. The lake, the music, the temple's reflection—it was all like a perfect dream, a place where nature, spirituality, and humanity came together in harmony. We left feeling deeply connected not only to the beauty of Bali but to the people we had met along the way, each one adding a new layer to our journey.

As the morning light began to dance more brightly across the landscape, we geared up for our next destination: a hidden waterfall known as Banyumala. The thought of a secluded waterfall tucked away in Bali's lush jungle landscape filled us with excitement, and even a bit of nervous anticipation. We had heard that reaching Banyumala wasn't an easy feat—it required navigating steep trails and rocky paths, and a car wouldn't be able to handle the terrain. So, we decided to rent a motorbike for the journey and found ourselves introduced to Ketut, our driver, who was as much a guide as he was a storyteller.

Ketut was an older Balinese man, perhaps in his sixties, with a warm smile and a twinkle in his eye that spoke of years of adventure. His easy-going laugh was contagious, and we immediately felt at ease as he adjusted our helmets and assured us, "Don't worry, you're in safe hands. I've been driving these trails since I was a boy." Ketut's confidence made us feel secure, though the rugged path ahead hinted that this would be no ordinary ride.

As we mounted the motorbike, Ketut shared little anecdotes about his childhood in the nearby villages, explaining how he'd often helped his family with farming, carrying goods along similar jungle paths to reach the local markets. "These trails," he laughed, "are like old friends to me. Every rock and tree have been here longer than I have." We couldn't help but be charmed by his deep connection to the land, and his knowledge of Bali's backroads reassured us as we set off into the forest.

The path was a wild ride—Ketut skilfully maneuvered the motorbike over rocky patches, through narrow turns, and up steep inclines with an ease that seemed almost magical. At times, the trail hugged the edge of the jungle so closely that branches brushed against us, and the thick, earthy scent of the forest filled the air. Krittika, who held on to me tightly from behind, let out occasional gasps and laughs each time we hit a bump. Ketut would just chuckle softly and call back, “Hold on tight! It’s part of the adventure!”

As we ventured deeper into the wilderness, the sounds of the world began to change. Instead of the distant hum of traffic or bustling crowds, we heard only the rustling of leaves, the call of birds, and the faint gurgle of a nearby stream. After a while, the faint sound of rushing water began to grow louder, and Ketut slowed the bike, pulling over in a small clearing. “We’re here,” he announced with a grin, gesturing toward a hidden path that led into the dense undergrowth.

We followed Ketut down the narrow trail, which wound its way through lush greenery and tangled vines. Each step brought us closer to the waterfall, the sound of the water growing louder until it felt like a living presence all around us. And then, as we rounded a final bend, Banyumala Falls appeared before us. The sight was nothing short of magical—cascading down a series of rocky cliffs, the water seemed to glow in the dappled sunlight, falling gracefully into a clear pool at the base. Mist rose from the water, catching the morning light and casting a soft, ethereal glow over the scene.

Krittika and I were speechless. The falls seemed untouched by time, a hidden paradise nestled away from the world, and we couldn’t quite believe we were lucky enough to witness it. Ketut, noticing our awe, quietly said, “Banyumala is special, yes? Not many people come here. It’s a gift from nature.” His words were filled with a reverence that made the moment feel even more sacred, as if we were being entrusted with a secret.

The air was cool and fresh, invigorated by the mist rising from the falls, and as we sat by the edge of the pool, dipping our feet into the clear, refreshing water, an overwhelming sense of peace washed over us. It felt as if we had left the modern world behind and entered a sanctuary belonging solely to nature. The powerful rhythm of the waterfall blended with the sounds of the forest, creating a harmony that seemed to resonate deep within us. We felt as if we were part of something ancient and timeless, surrounded by the life of the jungle, each creature and plant connected in an intricate web of existence.

After a while, we couldn't resist the allure of the water. Krittika slipped off her shoes, laughing as she waded into the shallows, the coolness sending a delightful shiver up her spine. "It's incredible!" she called, her voice echoing slightly against the rocks. I joined her, and we spent several minutes just standing there, letting the water lap against our legs, laughing and savoring the pure, untouched beauty of the place.

Ketut, sensing our awe, murmured, "Banyumala is special because few people come here. It's a gift from nature, yes?"

We nodded in silent awe, each of us struck by the profound beauty of Banyumala Waterfall. It was as if words were inadequate for what lay before us—a place that seemed woven from dreams and nature's purest elements. The cool air felt alive, charged with the mist rising from the cascading water and filling our lungs with its crisp freshness. We settled down by the edge of the crystal-clear pool, the coolness of the water meeting our feet with a gentle shock that only heightened the feeling of connection to this hidden paradise. It was more than a picturesque scene; it was a deep, humbling sense of peace, as if we had stumbled upon a sacred corner of the world, untouched by time or disruption.

The forest around us was alive, a symphony of subtle sounds—the distant chirping of unseen birds, the whisper of leaves rustling in the soft breeze, and the powerful, rhythmic roar of the waterfall. Each sound melded into a natural harmony that stilled our minds, dissolving any lingering thoughts or worries. We felt cradled by the ancient trees, sheltered by the towering cliffs, and soothed by the constant, grounding rhythm of the water. In that quiet sanctuary, all that mattered was the present moment—a fragile yet eternal connection to nature.

At length, Ketut gave us a gentle nod, signalling that it was time to leave. With reluctant hearts and grateful spirits, we rose, casting one last, lingering look at Banyumala. It was difficult to pull ourselves away, as if part of our spirits had rooted themselves to this magical spot. We climbed back up the trail, carrying with us an invisible but profound memory of the waterfall's beauty and its quiet, sacred energy—a gift from Bali that we would hold close forever.

By midday, hunger reminded us of the need to refuel, so we stopped at a small roadside café and ordered some local fare. The owner, Wayan, greeted us with a cheerful "Selamat siang!" as she prepared our food. The café was simple and cozy, its bamboo walls decorated with local crafts and family photos. She brought us chicken burgers served with rice and a tangy chili sauce, and as we ate, she shared stories about her family and her life in the area.

"We've lived here for generations," she told us with a proud smile. "Tourists come and go, but we are always here. This is our home."

Her words resonated deeply with us, grounding us in the timelessness of Bali's traditions and the strong sense of community that seemed to permeate every corner of the island.

Finally, we made our way to Kintamani, where we had rented an Airbnb overlooking the breathtaking Lake Batur. The road twisted and turned as it climbed higher into the mountains, each curve revealing sweeping views of the shimmering lake below, surrounded by the volcanic peaks of Mount Batur and Mount Agung. As we ascended, the air grew cooler, a refreshing change from the tropical heat of the lowlands.

Our Airbnb was a hidden gem, a charming wooden cabin perched on the edge of a lush hillside, offering an unobstructed view of the serene lake below and the towering mountains in the distance. The cabin itself was a cozy haven, its rustic design blending seamlessly with the natural surroundings. Inside, large windows framed the breathtaking landscape, inviting the beauty of Bali's highlands into every room. Stepping onto the balcony, we were greeted by a cool, refreshing breeze that carried the scent of the surrounding trees and the earth, making the air feel impossibly fresh.

From the balcony, the view before us was simply mesmerizing—the lake, calm and mirror-like, stretched out below, its surface kissed by the soft morning mist that seemed to rise like smoke from the water. The mountains, with their mist-covered peaks, stood as silent sentinels in the distance, their towering presence giving a sense of timelessness to the scene. The sound of nature—the gentle rustling of leaves, the occasional chirp of birds—was all we could hear, and it felt as though the world had slowed down, allowing us to fully absorb the peacefulness of the moment.

As evening began to fall, the sky transformed into a breathtaking canvas, shifting from shades of soft pink to deep blues and purples, as if the heavens themselves were painting a masterpiece. The golden light of the setting sun cast a warm glow over the landscape, reflecting on the still surface of the lake and creating a stunning contrast with the darkening mountains. It was a scene of such tranquillity and beauty that it almost felt unreal, like a moment suspended in time.

Wrapped in blankets, we sat together on the balcony, content in the stillness that surrounded us. The world seemed so far away, and for those few hours, it felt as if we were the only people on Earth. The peace of the place seeped deep into our hearts, and we shared a quiet conversation, feeling deeply connected not only to each other but to the land itself. The silence, punctuated only by the occasional distant sound of nature, enveloped us, and we let it settle over us like a comforting embrace, knowing that this moment—this perfect sense of serenity—would stay with us long after we left this magical place.

Our hosts had prepared a feast that night, a comforting meal of chicken stew simmered with fragrant herbs and spices, paired with an array of barbecued vegetables. The stew was hearty and warm, each bite carrying the deep flavours of Bali's unique spice blend, and the vegetables had been grilled to smoky perfection, their natural sweetness enhanced by the gentle char. It was more than a meal; it was a taste of Bali's warmth and a reminder of the care and hospitality woven into the island's culture. We ate slowly, savoring each bite, the rich flavours perfectly complementing the cozy ambiance of the cabin.

Outside, the world seemed suspended in stillness, as if the mountains themselves were keeping watch over our evening. The only sounds were the faint rustling of leaves carried by the cool mountain breeze and the occasional crackle from the fireplace inside. The quiet added a layer of intimacy to the meal, a tranquil backdrop that made us feel completely removed from the rest of the world.

After dinner, we wrapped ourselves in blankets and wandered onto the balcony again, drawn by the night's clear sky. The stars were luminous, scattered across the heavens with such brilliance that they seemed almost within reach. We stood in awe, gazing up at the sky, breathing in the crisp mountain air tinged with the earthy scents of nature. The silence around us was profound, filling us with a sense of peace that was both grounding and expansive. We felt a powerful connection—to each other, to this beautiful island, and to the universe that seemed to enfold us in its vast, starlit embrace.

In that serene, starlit moment, Bali felt less like a distant destination and more like a familiar friend, a part of us that would stay long after our return. As we finally drifted off to sleep that night, the quiet of the mountains settled around us like a soft lullaby, and we knew that this place, this island, was now woven into the fabric of our lives. This journey had been more than a honeymoon; it had become a discovery, a testament to love, and a heartfelt thank-you to the island that had shown us so much wonder.

Chapter 5: Into the Heart of the Volcano

March 9, 2024

The dead of night surrounded us, the world blanketed in darkness as we stirred awake. The clock read only 2 a.m., yet sleep was nowhere to be found. Outside, the air lay thick with silence, save for the occasional rustling of leaves in the cool, crisp mountain breeze. There was a chill in the air that bit through our blankets, sharper than usual in the high-altitude stillness. We layered up in warm clothes, the excitement of our early start tingling in our veins and outweighing the call to stay in the comfort of bed.

Today, we were setting off on one of Bali's most cherished adventures—the journey to the summit of Mount Batur, an active volcano that has watched over Bali for centuries. Our plan was ambitious yet exhilarating: to reach the peak by sunrise, where we'd witness a spectacle of light and colour that Bali is renowned for. The thought of standing on that mountaintop, high above the waking world, filled us with both awe and nervous energy.

We gathered our things, double-checked our gear, and with a final deep breath, we stepped out into the predawn quiet. The night wrapped around us, and under a sky dotted faintly with stars, we began our adventure, guided by only the dim glow of our flashlight and the promise of an unforgettable dawn at Bali's edge.

Our 4x4 jeep soon rumbled up to the Airbnb, its headlights slicing through the darkness. Our guide, a young Balinese man named Arjuna, stepped out to greet us, his face lit by a warm smile.

"Ready for some adventure?" he asked, eyes twinkling even in the dark with a smile on his lips.

"Absolutely!" I replied, trying to contain my excitement.

As we climbed into the jeep, the engine roared to life, and we were off, plunging deeper into the night as we made our way toward the mountain. The road was rough, each bump and jolt heightening our anticipation. We wound our way up the rugged terrain, the dark shapes of trees and cliffs looming around us as the jeep navigated the narrow path. Occasionally, the headlights would catch a glimpse of the volcanic landscape, casting strange shadows over the rocky ground. It was eerie yet exhilarating—a feeling that we were embarking on an ancient pilgrimage into the very heart of the Earth.

Arjuna, catching the gleam of excitement in our eyes, smiled knowingly and began to share a piece of Mount Batur's story that stretched far beyond its volcanic nature. "Mount Batur is one of Bali's most sacred mountains," he began, his voice gentle yet reverent. He paused to gaze up at the silhouette of the peak against the night sky, as if the mountain itself could hear him. "For the Balinese, Batur is not just a mountain; it's a place of spirit, power, and deep respect. People have lived here around its base for centuries, in awe of it, knowing it can bring both life and destruction."

He went on, explaining how Batur has erupted many times over the years, shaping not only the landscape but the lives of those who live in its shadow. "It's been active for thousands of years, and it still erupts from time to time, though not as often as it once did," he said with a slight nod. "Our ancestors would offer prayers here, seeking protection, honouring the spirits that they believed lived within the volcano. Even today, we hold ceremonies for Batur to respect its power and give thanks."

Arjuna's words lingered in the air, a mixture of reverence and caution that made us feel the weight of the journey we were about to take. "For us," he continued, his eyes bright in the dark, "Batur is both feared and respected. It's a reminder of nature's strength, and a guardian, watching over Bali with a kind of quiet wisdom." We listened, absorbing each word, feeling ourselves drawn deeper into Bali's spirit and the unique reverence the island holds for places like Batur. The adventure ahead seemed to take on a whole new significance as we glanced up at the towering shadow of the mountain, feeling the presence of the countless souls who had once stood where we were, eyes lifted toward the peak in awe and wonder.

We reached a point where the jeep could go no farther, so we disembarked and started the final leg of our journey on foot. The night was so dark that our flashlights barely cut through it, but Arjuna led us forward with a confident stride, clearly familiar with every step of the path.

As we climbed higher, the chill in the air intensified, wrapping around us with an icy grip that made us shiver beneath our layers. Each gust of wind cut through the darkness like a knife, carrying with it the sharp, earthy scent of sulphur that reminded us of the volcano's raw, untamed power beneath our feet. The wind seemed to grow stronger with each step, swirling around us and tugging at our jackets as if testing our resolve.

With every exhale, our breaths materialized in frosty, wispy puffs that floated briefly in the beams of our flashlights before vanishing into the dark. It felt surreal, as if we were trekking through some enchanted, otherworldly landscape far removed from the warm beaches and lush jungles of Bali below. I reached for Krittika's hand, finding reassurance in her firm, warm grip. We walked in silence for a while, seeming like the comfort of each other's presence, each step forward a small act of courage as we made our way toward the summit.

The path grew steeper and more rugged, each rocky incline demanding our focus and strength. The climb was challenging, testing not just our stamina but our determination to reach the top. But with each stumble, each slip of the foot on loose gravel, we steadied ourselves, looking up to see how far we had come. And through it all, the thought of reaching the summit—of standing on that peak and watching the world awaken beneath a fiery sunrise—pulled us onward. It was that quiet promise, that anticipation of a moment so powerful, that kept us going, step by careful step, through the darkness.

Finally, as we neared the top, we saw the faintest hint of dawn breaking on the horizon. The dark blue sky was beginning to lighten, streaked with shades of purple and indigo. Just as we reached the summit, the sun began to rise, spilling light over the island in a wave of breathtaking beauty.

The view was unlike anything we had ever seen. In one direction, the sun rose, a burning orb casting a warm, golden glow across the landscape. It painted the clouds in shades of pink and orange, turning the entire sky into a canvas of colors. In the other direction, the shadows of the valley below stretched out, dark and mysterious. From this height, we could see Lake Batur shimmering in the early light, bordered by dense green forests and the jagged edges of ancient lava flows. The entire island seemed to be waking up beneath us, each peak and valley coming alive in the morning light.

"Oh my god," Krittika whispered, her voice full of wonder.

I was speechless, my heart pounding as I took it all in. The vastness of the scene, the way the mountains rolled into the distance, the surreal beauty of the sun rising over an active volcano—this was more than just a view; it was an experience that felt spiritual, as though we were part of something much larger than ourselves.

Arjuna noticed our awe and nodded knowingly. "This is why we climb," he said simply. "The sunrise here—it reminds us that no matter what happens, each day is a gift."

As the sun slowly rose, its first golden rays stretched across the summit, casting a warm glow over the rugged landscape. The chill that had clung to us during the climb began to melt away, replaced by a gentle warmth that seemed to reach right into our souls. Standing there, surrounded by the vastness of the mountain and the sweeping view of the land below, we felt a deep, almost reverent connection—to the mountain, to the island of Bali, and to each other. It was as if the peak itself, ancient and wise, had granted us permission to witness something sacred and enduring.

We found ourselves instinctively slowing down, drawn into the beauty that stretched in every direction. The world was awake now, bathed in sunlight, with the mist lifting to reveal distant hills, valleys, and the shimmering lake far below. Each scene was like a painting, colours shifting and deepening as the sun rose higher.

We spent several minutes in silence, just absorbing it all, letting each sight and sound imprint on our minds. Though we took pictures, eagerly capturing the memory to look back on, we made a conscious effort to put down the camera and simply *be*. We wanted to feel this moment with all our senses—the warmth of the sun, the scent of the volcanic earth, the soft whispers of the breeze, and the quiet strength we felt standing there together. In those precious moments, time felt suspended, and it was as if the mountain itself had woven its spirit into our memory, a bond we knew we would carry with us always.

Once we had taken in the breathtaking sunrise, Arjuna led us down a different path, guiding us toward the ash fields that surrounded the mighty Mount Batur. As we descended, the landscape shifted in a way that left us almost speechless. Gone were the vibrant, golden hues of dawn, and in their place was a stark, dramatic contrast. The lush greenery of Bali's forests, which had seemed so abundant and alive just moments ago, now gave way to shades of black, grey, and deep charcoal. The ground beneath our feet was covered in thick volcanic ash, which stretched out in every direction like a barren desert that seemed to belong to no world we knew. It was as if we had stepped into an entirely different realm—an alien landscape so otherworldly that it almost felt surreal.

The ash fields had a heavy stillness to them, broken only by the occasional whisper of the wind stirring the fine particles of ash that drifted lazily in the air. With each step, we left behind an imprint in the soft, yet gritty earth, and small clouds of dust erupted beneath our feet, floating briefly before disappearing into the quiet. The landscape felt strangely ghostly, as though we were walking through a place that had been untouched by time, or perhaps frozen in a moment of volcanic eruption that had left its mark for centuries. The ash, dark and thick, clung to everything it touched—our shoes, our clothing, and even the air we breathed. The atmosphere felt heavy, yet oddly peaceful, as if the mountain, in all its power, was holding its breath.

Despite the silence, there was an undeniable energy here—raw and powerful, a palpable reminder of the volcano's constant presence beneath the surface. Walking through the fields, we could feel the earth vibrating with that energy, the weight of centuries of volcanic activity simmering just below our feet. The contrast between the fertile, vibrant forests of Bali and these desolate, volcanic plains was striking, highlighting the delicate balance between nature's lush beauty and its raw, untamed forces. The stillness was mesmerizing, but it also left us with a sense of awe, knowing that the mountain was alive in a way we had never quite understood before. It felt as though we were walking in the shadow of something far larger than ourselves, something that could both create and destroy, as it had for generations.

Krittika looked around in awe, her eyes wide. "This feels like… a movie set or something," she said. "It's so stark but beautiful."

Arjuna, sensing our fascination, explained, "These fields were created by past eruptions. Batur's lava flows covered this area, leaving behind the ash and rocks you see now. It's a reminder of the volcano's power."

The further we ventured into the ash fields, the more isolated and eerily quiet it became. The landscape seemed to stretch on endlessly, with no sign of life except for the occasional gust of wind that swept through, sending a fine mist of ash swirling into the air. The mountains, dark and imposing, stood like silent sentinels in the distance, their jagged peaks piercing the sky. There was a sense of both foreboding and awe in the way they dominated the horizon, as though they had been there long before us, and would remain long after we were gone. Every so often, we caught sight of wisps of smoke curling upward from small volcanic vents in the ground, like faint whispers of Mount Batur's ongoing vitality. These subtle signs of activity reminded us that the volcano, though calm in this moment, was still a living, breathing force, ready to erupt again at any time.

Standing there, surrounded by the dark, volcanic rock and the endless expanse of ash, we couldn't help but feel a deep, humbling sense of awe. It was as though the landscape itself was a testament to the immense power of nature—a reminder that the earth had been shaped, not by gentle hands, but by fire and force. The very ground beneath our feet, though soft and gritty with ash, held the imprint of thousands of years of eruptions, each one leaving behind its mark on the land. We were visitors here, small and transient in comparison to the ancient forces that had shaped this place. The air was thick with the scent of sulphur, a constant reminder that beneath the stillness, the volcano's energy was still churning, alive and restless.

As we walked deeper into the fields, the weight of the silence around us grew more profound. The ash crunched beneath our boots with every step, and the vast emptiness made us feel as though we were the only two people in the world. The sun, now higher in the sky, cast long shadows across the barren landscape, illuminating the jagged rocks and sparse vegetation that somehow managed to survive in such a harsh environment. Despite the beauty of the view, there was a rawness to the scene that stirred something primal within us. It was humbling to be surrounded by such stark reminders of the earth's immense power, and we found ourselves deeply aware of how fleeting our presence here was in the grand scale of time. We were but brief witnesses to a landscape that had been moulded by millennia of volcanic activity, shaped by fire and fury, and yet still holding the quiet resilience of something ancient and enduring.

At one point, Arjuna picked up a handful of ash, letting it sift through his fingers as he said, "This ash is sacred to us. It's a reminder of both creation and destruction. Life and death, side by side."

We watched in silence, moved by the weight of his words, as the ash scattered into the wind.

The morning wore on, and as the sun climbed higher, the shadows began to fade, leaving the ash fields bathed in bright light. We spent hours exploring, capturing photos, and simply marvelling at the unique beauty of this volcanic landscape. By 10 a.m., it was time to head back, our minds and hearts full from the unforgettable experience.

As we made our way back down the mountain, I looked over at Krittika, who was still gazing out over the ash fields, lost in thought. This journey had been unlike anything we'd ever done before—a sunrise over a live volcano, the otherworldly ash fields, the quiet yet immense power of Mount Batur. It was an adventure we would carry with us, a memory etched not only in our minds but also in our souls.

With the morning behind us and the warmth of the sun on our backs, we returned to the jeep, ready to descend from Mount Batur, forever changed by the magic and majesty we had experienced.

Chapter 6: From Coffee Beans to Canyon Waters

March 9, 2024

After our unforgettable morning on Mount Batur, we turned our sights toward Sidemen, a serene and lesser-known corner of Bali that promised peacefulness and an authentic glimpse into the island's timeless charm. Often overshadowed by the bustling tourist hubs, Sidemen is a place where the heart of Bali beats at its own unhurried pace, surrounded by a tapestry of emerald-green rice terraces and rolling hills. It was a destination we had been eager to visit, a retreat from the crowds and a chance to connect with the raw beauty of the island.

The journey to Sidemen was itself a mesmerizing experience, as if the drive were an invitation to a dreamscape. The narrow roads wound gently through the lush countryside, flanked on either side by rice paddies that seemed to stretch endlessly, their terraces cascading like green waves across the landscape. The early afternoon light played on the water-soaked fields, creating a shimmering effect that made the paddies appear alive, rippling under the caress of the soft breeze. In the distance, mist-shrouded mountains loomed, their outlines hazy yet majestic, standing as silent guardians of the land below.

Every turn in the road brought a new surprise—a quaint village here, a hidden temple there. Farmers, dressed in traditional sarongs and conical hats, worked the fields with a quiet diligence, their figures bent over as they planted or harvested rice. Occasionally, we passed women carrying towering baskets of offerings on their heads, their graceful movements a reflection of Bali's spiritual rhythm. At one point, we stopped to watch a group of children playing by a small stream, their laughter ringing out like music that harmonized perfectly with the natural surroundings. They waved enthusiastically as we drove by, their smiles a reminder of the warmth and simplicity that permeates Balinese life.

The air grew fresher as we ventured further from the bustling towns, filled with the earthy scent of damp soil and the faint sweetness of blooming flowers. We rolled down the windows to let it all in, and Krittika leaned out slightly, her hair catching the breeze as she gazed at the scenery with wonder. "It's like stepping back in time," she said softly, her voice full of admiration. I could only nod in agreement, as words felt inadequate to describe the sheer beauty that surrounded us.

Small roadside stalls dotted the journey, selling everything from tropical fruits to woven baskets and wooden carvings. At one such stall, we stopped to buy fresh coconuts. The vendor, an elderly man with a kind face, expertly hacked off the top of a coconut and handed it to us with a broad smile. "Selamat jalan," he said, wishing us a safe journey as we sipped the sweet, refreshing water. It was moments like these—unassuming yet heartfelt—that made the journey feel as meaningful as the destination itself.

As we continued, the landscape became even more dramatic, with the rice terraces rising and falling in perfect harmony with the contours of the land. The play of light and shadow added depth to the scene, making it appear almost like a painting brought to life. It was impossible not to feel awestruck by the artistry of both nature and the farmers who had shaped this land over generations, their work a testament to the enduring bond between the Balinese people and the earth.

As we strolled past the entrance of the coffee plantation, something about the rich, earthy aroma and the lush green surroundings drew us in. We glanced at each other, our curiosity sparked. Almost on impulse, we made a sudden decision to veer off the main path and explore the plantation garden. The rows of coffee plants stretched out before us, their broad leaves glistening in the morning light. We drove the car slowly, admiring the vibrant greenery and the careful layout of the garden, where coffee plants, cocoa trees, and exotic herbs grew side by side. Here and there, small signs described the plants and the unique ways they contribute to the local flavours and culture. Venturing deeper, we noticed the civet enclosures, where the shy, nocturnal animals rested in shaded corners. The quiet hum of nature filled the air, and for a moment, we felt as if we'd stumbled upon a hidden world, where every plant and animal played a part in Bali's treasured coffee tradition.

Our first stop on the way was to try the famed Kopi Luwak, or as it's famously known, "poop coffee." This rare and unique coffee is made from beans that have been eaten and passed by the civet cat, a small, nocturnal animal native to the region. The civet's digestive enzymes are said to alter the beans, enhancing their flavour and creating a distinctly smooth, rich brew. As we reached the small, rustic coffee plantation, our curiosity grew alongside a touch of hesitation. A friendly guide welcomed us, explaining the intricate process that makes Kopi Luwak so special. He showed us where the civet cats lived and how the beans were carefully collected, cleaned, and roasted.

As we entered the small coffee plantation, the scent of freshly roasted coffee filled the air. We were welcomed by a young gardener with a warm smile and a kind demeanour. She spoke limited English, so we used Google Translate to communicate, laughing as we stumbled through translations. Her enthusiasm, however, needed no translation.

She led us to a small wooden hut where we could see the entire coffee-making process, from the lush green plants to the beans harvested by hand. Her eyes lit up as she explained each step, speaking quickly in her local dialect, pausing for us to translate. She showed us how the civet cats eat the coffee cherries and how the beans are carefully cleaned and roasted to remove any remaining acidity and bitterness.

"It's like the civet cat gives us a gift," she said through translation, her eyes shining. "It makes the coffee taste smooth, not bitter."

We watched, fascinated, as she expertly ground the roasted beans and brewed a pot of the aromatic coffee. When she poured it into small cups for us, the dark, rich liquid shimmered in the sunlight, filling the air with a deep, earthy aroma. We took a tentative sip and were immediately surprised—the coffee was incredibly smooth, with a hint of sweetness and a nutty, slightly caramelized aftertaste. It was unlike any coffee we'd ever tasted.

The young gardener watched our reactions, beaming. "You like?" she asked with a hopeful smile, not needing translation for this question.

"Yes, it's amazing!" Krittika replied, nodding enthusiastically. The girl grinned, pleased that we were enjoying something so special to her.

After our coffee, we thanked her with a heartfelt "Terima kasih," and she waved goodbye as we continued on our journey, both touched by the simple kindness of the people we had met.

Our next stop was the famous Tukad Cepung waterfall, one of Bali's hidden gems. Known for its mesmerizing beauty, this waterfall lay tucked within a secluded canyon, where nature had crafted a spectacular skylight effect. Sunlight poured through narrow openings at the top, filtering down to illuminate the canyon walls with warm, radiant beams that seemed to dance as we moved. The entrance was marked by imposing rock walls that towered above us, their surfaces blanketed in moss and trailing vines that added a sense of timelessness to the place.

As we ventured down the winding, narrow path, the air grew cooler and more humid, filled with the earthy scent of wet stone and foliage. The faint sounds of rushing water began to grow louder with each step, echoing off the canyon walls and creating an enchanting resonance that guided us forward like nature's own call.

The pathway leading deeper into the canyon felt like stepping into an enchanted forest. Dense, lush greenery flanked both sides of the narrow trail, with thick ferns sprawling out in rich, layered shades of green. Moss covered nearly every rock, giving them an almost velvety texture, while clusters of delicate wildflowers peeked through the undergrowth. As we pressed on, the space around us grew tighter, the rock walls on either side seeming to gently close in, wrapping us in a quiet, secluded embrace.

Soft rays of sunlight filtered down through small cracks and openings above, scattering across the pathway in delicate patterns and casting a subtle, ethereal glow over everything. It felt as though the canyon was alive with hidden magic, as if nature itself had crafted this spot for those willing to venture into its depths. The faint rustle of leaves and the distant birdsong added a gentle rhythm to the environment, blending harmoniously with the growing roar of the waterfall just ahead. Each step brought us nearer, and soon the refreshing coolness of the mist began to kiss our skin, mingling with the earthy scent of damp rock and fresh foliage, invigorating our senses with each breath.

Finally, we reached the waterfall itself. The water cascaded down the rock face, tumbling over dark stones in a translucent sheet. Sunlight poured in from above, creating beams of light that sliced through the mist, making the entire space feel almost surreal. We stood there, entranced by the sight, the sunlight playing off the water droplets like scattered crystals. The natural beauty of the scene was overwhelming, and for a few moments, we simply stood in silence, soaking it all in.

What made this waterfall so otherworldly was the way the sun's rays pierced through the narrow gaps in the canyon above, casting beams of golden light that cut through the mist like rays of hope. These shafts of sunlight danced on the surface of the water, making it sparkle as if the waterfall itself were alive, shimmering with energy. The surrounding rocks, blackened by time and water, were adorned with patches of moss and ferns, adding layers of green to the already vibrant landscape.

The cliffs, towering like ancient guardians, seemed to embrace the waterfall, their jagged edges softened by the vibrant greenery that clung to them. The spray of the water created an ever-present mist, giving the entire scene a mystical quality, as though this hidden sanctuary were a secret oasis untouched by time. The rhythm of the waterfall's rush was hypnotic, lulling us into a trance, while the occasional calls of birds overhead added a symphonic touch to the melody of the water.

It felt as though we had stepped into a cinematic moment, where everything around us was bathed in a soft-focus glow—nature's grand performance on the world's stage. The beauty of Tukad Cepung was not just in its visual splendour but in the way it made us feel—small, humble, yet profoundly connected to something far greater than ourselves.

As we walked around, we met a few other travellers, each of them just as mesmerized by the beauty of Tukad Cepung as we were. An Australian couple nearby struck up a conversation with us, exchanging stories about the best spots they'd found in Bali.

"Isn't this place incredible?" the woman said, gesturing to the waterfall. "It's like something out of a dream."

We couldn't agree more. This secluded canyon waterfall, hidden away from the hustle and bustle of the city, felt like one of Bali's best-kept secrets—a little pocket of paradise.

With hearts full of wonder, we continued on to our final destination for the day: our Airbnb in Sideman. As we arrived, a young woman greeted us at the entrance, her face lighting up with a welcoming smile. She spoke English fluently and introduced herself as Made.

As we arrived at our Airbnb in Sidemen, the scene that greeted us felt like a frame lifted straight out of a movie. Nestled at the heart of Bali's untouched countryside, the retreat was a tranquil sanctuary, surrounded by a lush embrace of greenery that stretched as far as the eye could see. The air was alive with the fragrance of wet earth and fresh foliage, carrying the earthy scent of rain-soaked hills and the sweetness of nearby rice paddies.

The house itself, a charming wooden cabin, stood at the edge of a rolling hillside, its large windows offering panoramic views of the natural wonders that lay beyond. From every angle, we were enveloped by the beauty of the land—gentle, sloping hills cradled the home, covered in dense forest and occasional glimpses of hidden waterfalls cascading down the mountainside. The sound of the water rushing down the rocks mingled with the soft rustle of the trees, creating a symphony of nature that played out in perfect harmony.

Above us, the sky was an ever-changing canvas, painted with swirling clouds that lazily drifted across the expanse. They moved in slow motion, at times obscuring the sun, then parting to let the golden rays spill over the landscape. The clouds were like rolling cotton, soft and billowy, making the world feel like a dreamscape—timeless and serene.

Surrounding the house were the iconic, terraced rice fields of Sidemen, their vibrant green hues shining under the sun, like an artist's perfect brushstroke across the earth. The fields stretched out before us, their steps carved into the mountain, with the occasional worker walking through, adding to the pastoral charm. The vibrant rice plants, some still young, others ready for harvest, waved gently in the breeze, their golden tips glistening in the light.

It felt like we were living in a place untouched by time, a place where every element of nature came together in flawless symmetry—

greenery, hills, waterfalls, rice fields, and clouds—all blending into one cinematic masterpiece. The beauty was so palpable, so overwhelming, it seemed almost surreal, as though the world had crafted this perfect moment just for us. Each breath we took was a deep, grounding reminder of how deeply connected we were to this land, to this moment, and to the essence of Bali itself.

"Welcome!" she said warmly, "You're going to love it here." She led us to our wooden bungalow, nestled amidst the lush greenery with panoramic views of the surrounding hills and rice terraces.

As we settled in, Made noticed us admiring the view and began sharing stories about her love for Bollywood. "I am a huge fan of Shah Rukh Khan," she confessed, grinning shyly. "And the movie 'Kabhi Khushi Kabhie Gham'? I've watched it maybe twenty times!"

Krittika's face lit up with delight. "Oh, I love that movie too! It's a classic!"

We laughed, sharing favourite scenes and songs, feeling an instant bond over Bollywood. There was something special about connecting with people over shared interests, even halfway across the world.

Our bungalow itself was enchanting. Made entirely of wood, the interior had a rustic charm, and the large windows overlooked the scenic hills, bringing the beauty of Sideman right into our room. The bathroom was semi-open, blending indoor comfort with nature's tranquillity. As we explored our little haven, a light rain began to fall, the gentle patter creating a soothing symphony.

We ordered some pizza and local 'Bintang' beer for dinner, settling into the cozy space as the rain intensified outside. There was something magical about the moment—the sound of the rain, the scent of fresh wood, the mist rolling in from the mountains. We clinked our beer bottles together, toasting to another unforgettable day in Bali.

As we sat back in our cozy nook, the warmth of the pizza and the cool chill of the beer in our hands provided the perfect contrast to the gentle evening unfolding outside. The rain had begun to fall softly, at first just a light drizzle, but soon it turned into a steady cascade, each droplet tapping rhythmically against the windows. The vibrant greens of the landscape—the hills, the rice terraces, and the lush foliage—blurred as the rain painted the world outside with a soft, silvery sheen. It was as though the earth itself was being washed clean, transforming the scenery into a serene, misty painting that felt both serene and alive.

With each sip of beer, we could taste the refreshing coolness of the mountain air, which filtered in through the open window, carrying the earthy scent of rain-soaked soil and fresh plants. The cool breeze ruffled the edges of the curtains, filling the room with a sense of freshness that seemed to reset our minds and bodies. The rhythmic sound of the rain combined with the occasional rumble of distant thunder, creating a calming ambiance that soothed us into the present moment.

We ate slowly, relishing each bite of pizza, its flavours rich and satisfying, perfectly complementing the simplicity of the moment. The pizza, hot and delicious, was a simple indulgence, but in this setting, it felt like an experience—a moment of bliss that we wanted to stretch into eternity. The rain continued to fall in soft sheets, and the landscape outside seemed to become more intimate, more inviting, as if nature itself was sharing its quiet, peaceful embrace with us.

A deep sense of peace washed over us, a rare and profound stillness that only comes from being completely immersed in nature's embrace. Here, with the rain and the mountains and the misty landscape all around us, we could truly feel the world slowing down, allowing us to let go of everything and just be—together, in this perfect, fleeting moment.

That evening, we drifted off to sleep accompanied by one of nature's most soothing melodies—the gentle patter of raindrops on the wooden roof above us. It was as if the Balinese countryside was singing a lullaby, a rhythmic symphony that blended seamlessly with the soft rustling of leaves and the distant hum of crickets. The air was cool and carried the earthy scent of rain-soaked soil, a reminder of the nurturing touch of nature all around us.

The cozy warmth of our cabin provided the perfect cocoon, a haven from the world outside, as we nestled under soft blankets. Every detail of the day replayed in our minds—the stunning landscapes of Sidemen, the endless rice terraces that seemed to ripple like waves in the breeze, and the kindness of the people who had welcomed us into their world. This corner of Bali had offered us not only its beauty but also its soul, inviting us to slow down, breathe deeply, and simply be.

As the rain continued its steady rhythm, our hearts swelled with gratitude. Sidemen had embraced us with an authenticity that was both humbling and unforgettable. The simplicity of life here, combined with its natural magnificence, had left an indelible mark on our spirits. With each droplet of rain, it felt as though the land itself was whispering its blessings, leaving us with a profound sense of peace. As we closed our eyes, the world outside faded into a soft blur, and we drifted into dreams filled with the verdant greens of Bali, the laughter of its people, and the serenity of its countryside. We knew that Sidemen had given us a gift—memories we would carry with us always, etched not just in our minds but in our hearts, a gentle reminder of a place where life and nature harmonized so effortlessly.

Chapter 7: Gateways to Heaven and Dancing Demons

March 10, 2024

"In Sidemen's arms, where green hills breathe,

A serene world lies, the heart finds reprieve.

Terraces ripple, like emerald seas,

Dancing in tune with the soft mountain breeze."

- *Krittika*

The morning in Sidemen unfolded like a scene from a dream, as if the very earth itself was gently waking up to greet us. Stepping out onto the balcony of our wooden bungalow, we were greeted by a sight that felt like stepping into a living painting. The sky was swathed in a veil of mist, soft clouds hanging low over the emerald hills, their edges catching the golden glow of the sun still hidden behind the mountains. The light was delicate, diffused by the mist, casting a serene glow over the terraced rice fields that stretched endlessly below, glistening with the remnants of dawn's dew.

The air was cool and refreshing, filled with the faint aroma of dew-kissed leaves and the rich, earthy scent of fertile soil. Each breath felt like a tonic, a connection to the untouched coolness of this lush countryside. The soundscape was equally soothing—a symphony of rustling palm fronds, chirping birds, and the faint trickle of a distant stream meandering its way through the valley.

We stood there in awe, watching as the morning light gradually intensified, gently lifting the mist to reveal the vibrant hues of green that blanketed the hills. The rice paddies glistened like mirrors, reflecting the awakening sky and the first hints of the sun. It was a moment of pure stillness and wonder, as if time itself had slowed to honour the beauty of Sidemen's morning. This wasn't just a view; it was an experience that touched the soul, a moment of perfect harmony between nature and our own hearts.

From our vantage point, we could see the vast expanse of the valley below, where emerald rice fields stretched like an intricate patchwork quilt, woven together by winding rivers and small, hidden villages. The hillsides, lush and verdant, seemed to rise and fall like gentle waves, their peaks veiled by the mist that lazily drifted across the land. The scene felt timeless, as if the world had paused just for us to experience this quiet beauty in perfect stillness.

After a hearty breakfast, we felt our spirits lift in anticipation. The warmth of freshly brewed Balinese coffee and the comfort of local delicacies left us energized and ready for the day's adventure. With eager hearts, we set off toward Lempuyang Temple, one of Bali's most sacred and iconic landmarks. The journey began with the hum of the engine beneath us as we drove through the winding roads, our path surrounded by lush green hillsides and pockets of dense forest. The mist hung low, shifting like a living thing, sometimes parting for a moment to reveal the awe-inspiring landscape, and then closing in again, shrouding everything in an enigmatic embrace.

The roads seemed to wind forever, curling around corners and dipping into hidden valleys where ancient temples peeked from behind trees, as if watching over the land for centuries. The air grew heavier with the mystery of the place, the damp earth beneath our tires muffling the sounds of the world, allowing only the whispers of the wind and the occasional bird call to break the silence. With every turn, the excitement in our hearts grew, knowing that we were about to experience not just a destination, but a journey into the heart of Bali's spiritual soul.

As we arrived at the temple parking lot, the quiet surroundings seemed to mirror the calmness of the place. We parked the car and made our way to the waiting temple shuttle bus, which was ready to take visitors up the winding path that led to the temple's base. The air felt different here—cooler, with a subtle weight to it, as though it carried an unseen energy. There was a calmness, but beneath that calm, a certain electric tension seemed to hum softly, something that sparked our curiosity but remained just beyond our understanding.

Climbing aboard the shuttle, we ascended slowly through the lush landscape, the path winding sharply up the mountainside, bordered by thick, dense trees and vibrant green vegetation. With each turn, the view of the surrounding valleys and hills expanded, offering fleeting glimpses of the hidden beauty of Bali's sacred land. The shuttle's gentle rumble on the uneven roads almost added to the sense of reverence, as if we were being guided into a space of deep spiritual significance.

When we arrived at the entrance to the temple, we were struck by the unexpected stillness. The place was surprisingly quiet, with only a handful of visitors milling about—a stark contrast to the typical crowds one would expect at such a renowned and iconic destination. The usual bustle of eager tourists snapping photos and chatting excitedly was absent. It was almost as if the temple itself had absorbed the usual throngs of people, leaving a hushed atmosphere that seemed to invite contemplation rather than curiosity.

As we stood there, taking in the rare solitude of the scene, the reason for the emptiness soon became clear. The towering gates of the temple, framed by moss-covered stone pillars, loomed ahead, shrouded in an almost mystical fog that had thickened in the morning air. This wasn't just any day at Lempuyang Temple—it was a special occasion, one that made our visit feel more like an intimate experience than a typical tourist stop.

As we approached the entrance to the temple, my attention was immediately drawn to a young Balinese boy sitting on a low stone wall near the gate. His wide, mischievous grin seemed to capture the very essence of youthful curiosity, and his eyes sparkled with an energy that was impossible to ignore. Intrigued, I walked over to him, and with a warm smile, I greeted him with a friendly "Selamat pagi!"—a simple "Good morning" in Indonesian.

His face immediately lit up at my greeting, and he responded with enthusiasm, eager to share what seemed to be a secret. His voice was filled with excitement as he explained that today was no ordinary day at Lempuyang Temple—it was the Ogoh Ogoh festival. His words were filled with pride, and as he spoke, it was clear that the festival held great meaning for him and for the entire Balinese community. He told us that this festival was an essential part of the celebrations leading up to Nyepi, the Balinese Day of Silence, which marks the start of the New Year in the Balinese Hindu calendar.

The Ogoh Ogoh festival, he explained, was a major event that took place the day before Nyepi, when the island was filled with a special kind of energy. The highlight of the festival was the elaborate parade featuring massive, intricately crafted statues made of bamboo and paper. These statues, he told us, represented various evil spirits and demons. The purpose of the parade—and the statues themselves—was to drive these negative energies away, purging the island and preparing it for the peaceful silence of Nyepi. The statues, often vivid and terrifying in their design, were meant to scare away the darkness, making way for renewal and spiritual cleansing.

His words painted a vivid picture in my mind of a vibrant and colorful celebration, where the streets would be filled with the sounds of music and chanting, with people joyously participating in the ritual to banish evil spirits. As he spoke, I could almost feel the excitement and reverence surrounding this sacred event, and for a moment, it felt as though we were on the cusp of witnessing something truly special. His energy was contagious, and I couldn't help but smile, grateful for this unexpected encounter that brought Bali's rich traditions to life in such a personal way.

“You’re lucky! Very lucky!” he said, gesturing with an animated wave. “Most people are with their families today, preparing for the festival tonight. That’s why the temple is so empty.”

We continued chatting, the boy’s light-hearted nature making us laugh with stories about mischievous ogoh ogoh statues and the village preparations. The connection we felt with him, despite our differences in culture, was heartwarming—a reminder of the shared humanity that transcends language and traditions.

After a while, he bid us goodbye, smiling widely and offering a cheerful wave as we headed up the stone steps. The temple itself is a place of reverence, its many layers and pagoda-like structures a reflection of the Balinese spiritual landscape. At the entrance, we were provided with sarongs—traditional Balinese skirts used to respectfully cover our legs, in accordance with temple customs. Wrapping ourselves in the flowing fabric, we felt even more connected to the ancient spiritual aura of the place.

After what felt like an otherworldly journey through the mist and the ancient temple grounds, we finally arrived at the iconic "Gateway of Heaven"—a sight that we had long dreamed of witnessing in person. As we stood before the grand stone gates, we were met with an awe-inspiring view that seemed almost too perfect to be real. The gates themselves were intricately carved, their weathered stones rising in elegant symmetry, forming a natural frame for the majestic silhouette of Mount Agung in the distance.

The mountain, Bali's most sacred peak, stood towering before us, its summit reaching skyward, piercing through a soft veil of clouds. The way the clouds wrapped themselves around the mountain, creating a halo of mist at its summit, gave the scene an ethereal, almost celestial quality. The air felt thick with reverence, and the combination of the striking stone arch and the breathtaking natural beauty of Mount Agung created a feeling of being suspended between two worlds—earthly and divine.

The colours of the scene were painted in soft, muted hues. The sky, streaked with pinks and oranges from the morning sun, gradually blended into the mist that clung to the mountain, adding a dreamlike quality to the entire scene. The verdant green fields below seemed to stretch endlessly, their vibrant colours contrasting against the rocky, snow-capped peak of Mount Agung.

We stood there for a long while, silently taking it all in, our breaths shallow and steady as if we didn't want to disturb the stillness that enveloped the space. Time seemed to slow in this sacred place, and we allowed ourselves to simply exist in the moment, with no rush, no need to speak. It was as though the universe itself had paused to give us this gift of peace—a deep, all-encompassing peace that radiated from the very heart of Bali.

The serenity of the moment was profound. There, in front of the "Gateway of Heaven," we felt a deep connection to the island and its spiritual essence, as though the natural world had reached out and wrapped us in its quiet, eternal embrace. We allowed the stillness to settle in our souls, grateful for the gift of being present in such a sacred space, a space where earth and sky met in perfect harmony.

Krittika and I posed for photos at the gateway, capturing the iconic image of the temple gates against the backdrop of Mount Agung. As we looked through the camera's lens, it felt like stepping into a postcard, the scene too beautiful to seem real. We soaked in the atmosphere, each moment spent here feeling both serene and surreal.

After spending a couple of hours at the temple, we reluctantly bid goodbye to Lempuyang and headed back toward the main road. By then, our stomachs were growling, so we stopped at a KFC nearby—a familiar name but with surprising differences. Not only was the menu slightly different, with flavours unique to Bali, but the prices were also much lower than what we were used to back home in India. We laughed, comparing notes on the subtle flavours and savouring the surprising novelty of fast food in Bali.

With our bellies full and spirits high, we left the bustling charm of the restaurant behind and made our way toward our next destination: Virgin Beach. Unlike the more well-known stretches of coastline, Virgin Beach was a hidden gem, tucked away from the usual throngs of tourists. Nestled between towering cliffs, the beach seemed to exist in its own secluded world, a tranquil escape from the hustle and bustle of Bali's more crowded spots. As we approached, the sense of exclusivity became palpable—the kind of place you might imagine only exists in postcards.

The landscape was a sight to behold. The sand, as white and fine as powdered sugar, stretched endlessly before us, an inviting expanse that seemed to sparkle under the soft sun. The water, an unbelievable shade of turquoise, shimmered in the sunlight, its clear surface revealing glimpses of coral beneath. As we walked closer, the soft waves gently lapped at the shore, their rhythmic motion creating a soothing soundtrack that seemed to add to the peaceful ambiance of the beach.

It was especially quiet today, as the ongoing Ogoh Ogoh festival had drawn many people away from the usual tourist attractions, leaving Virgin Beach almost entirely to ourselves. This rare moment of solitude felt like a luxury—an unspoiled slice of paradise where we could truly immerse ourselves in the beauty of Bali's coastline. The only sounds were the occasional whisper of the breeze moving through the palm trees and the distant crashing of waves against the rocky cliffs, enhancing the sense of isolation and calm that surrounded us.

We wandered along the shore, the soft sand slipping between our toes, feeling the cool breeze brush past us as we marvelled at the beauty of this untouched stretch of coastline. The cliffs that flanked the beach rose like natural sentinels, their dark rock faces contrasting beautifully with the white sand and the clear blue water. The lush vegetation that clung to the cliffs seemed to spill down toward the beach, adding an extra layer of vibrancy to the scene.

With the sun overhead casting its golden glow across the water, we sat on the sand for a while, simply absorbing the peace and natural beauty of Virgin Beach. It felt as though time itself had slowed down in this quiet, hidden sanctuary, and we were grateful for the rare privilege of experiencing it in its purest, most serene form. The perfect stillness of the moment allowed us to feel completely connected to the island, and we knew that Virgin Beach would forever be etched in our memories as one of Bali's most breathtaking and intimate places.

Changing into our swimsuits, a sense of excitement bubbled up between us. The temptation to dive into the crystal-clear waters was irresistible. As we stepped into the gentle surf, the cool water wrapped around our bodies, instantly refreshing in the tropical heat. The clarity of the water was incredible—it was so transparent that we could easily make out the soft sandy bottom beneath us, and tiny fish flitted about in the shallows, their scales glistening as they darted between the gentle ripples.

We waded deeper, our feet sinking slightly into the soft sand as the waves lapped against our legs. Then, with a shared glance, we plunged into the water, letting the ocean embrace us. The saltwater was refreshing, energizing, and as we swam through the cool expanse, it felt as though the whole world had slowed down. There was an unmatched sense of freedom in the open sea, each stroke taking us farther from the shore, where only the sound of our laughter and the rhythmic crash of the waves could be heard. The vastness of the ocean seemed to stretch endlessly in all directions, and for a moment, it was just us—floating, laughing, and feeling weightless in the embrace of this pristine paradise.

The waves, though gentle, provided just enough movement to make swimming and floating a blissful experience. We let ourselves be carried by the current, allowing the rhythm of the sea to soothe us. We playfully splashed each other, our laughter echoing over the water as we lost track of time. It was one of those rare moments when everything felt in perfect harmony—the warmth of the sun, the coolness of the water, the silence of the world around us, interrupted only by the sound of waves crashing softly onto the shore.

As we drifted back toward the shore, the sheer beauty of the place left us speechless. The beach stretched out behind us, its untouched expanse of white sand framed by the lush green cliffs, and the water was so clear that it seemed to glow with an inner light. Time, it seemed, had disappeared, replaced by the pure joy of the present moment, and we revelled in the simple pleasure of being completely immersed in such a breathtaking, peaceful place. Virgin Beach had become more than just a spot on the map—it was a moment of pure bliss, a memory we would carry with us long after we left.

As the afternoon wore on, we finally left Virgin Beach with happy hearts and sun-dappled skin, heading to our next Airbnb. Located near the village, this Airbnb was run by a German woman who greeted us warmly upon arrival. Her friendliness put us instantly at ease, and as we chatted, she shared her love for Bali and her passion for creating a welcoming space for travellers. Our bungalow was charming, made entirely of wood with large windows that opened to stunning views of the surrounding greenery. The bungalow was even two-storied, giving us plenty of space to relax and take in the tranquil atmosphere.

After freshening up, we decided to explore the Airbnb's bar, where we met a friendly bartender named Ketut. She was a young Balinese woman with an infectious smile, and she instantly engaged us in conversation.

"Have you heard about Ogoh Ogoh?" she asked, her eyes sparkling with excitement.

"Yes! We're actually planning to see the festival tonight!" Krittika replied.

Ketut's face instantly lit up with excitement as she began to share the story of her village's preparations for the night's festivities. Her eyes sparkled with enthusiasm, and her voice carried a rhythm of pride as she described the elaborate process of creating the *ogoh-ogoh* statues. These towering figures, she explained, were not just works of art—they were symbolic representations of demonic spirits, crafted specifically for the upcoming Ogoh-Ogoh Festival, which marked the eve of Nyepi, the Day of Silence.

She painted a vivid picture of the painstaking efforts involved in bringing these fearsome creatures to life. "Each *ogoh-ogoh* is a collaboration of the whole community," she said, gesturing toward the makeshift workshops scattered around the village. "Villagers gather materials like bamboo, which is flexible and strong, and then wrap them with layers of papier-mâché to form the body. The faces and details are painted with intricate designs, often featuring fierce expressions and exaggerated features—sharp fangs, wild eyes, and twisted horns."

Ketut's hands moved animatedly as she described the towering scale of these figures. "Some are as tall as seven to eight meters," she said with a smile, "so they need a lot of care and teamwork to build. It's a process that takes weeks, with every villager pitching in. The younger ones help with the painting, the elders guide the construction, and even the children carry pieces of bamboo to the workshops. It's a true labour of love."

She went on to explain the significance of these *ogoh-ogoh*, how they were meant to represent the evil spirits and negative energy that needed to be driven away before the sacred Day of Silence. "After the parade," she continued, "the statues are set on fire to symbolically burn away all the bad spirits, so the island and its people can start fresh for the new year. The flames symbolize purification." Ketut's eyes gleamed with pride as she spoke, and it was clear how deeply connected she was to these traditions—both in the ritual and the community effort behind them.

The joy and dedication she had for the celebration were palpable, and I could almost picture the village streets lit up with the warm glow of firelight, the air thick with the sounds of drums and the energy of hundreds of villagers moving in unison. It was a celebration of not only religious devotion but also community spirit, an intricate blend of culture, art, and ritual.

"Tonight, we'll dance, make noise, and bring out the ogoh-ogoh to scare away bad spirits before Nyepi," Ketut explained, her enthusiasm contagious.

As we chatted with Ketut and the other guests who had gathered at the bar, excitement built for the evening ahead. The festival felt like the culmination of everything we had come to love about Bali—its deep spirituality, vibrant culture, and the warmth of its people.

Later that night, we joined Ketut and a small group of other guests as we walked to the village square, where the festival had already begun. The scene was magical. Flickering torches lit the streets, and the villagers, dressed in traditional Balinese attire, gathered to watch the ogoh-ogoh statues. Each figure was more elaborate than the last, with bulging eyes, fangs, and brightly painted faces. As the music began—drums, cymbals, and gongs filling the air with rhythmic beats—the villagers lifted the statues onto their shoulders, chanting and dancing to scare away the evil spirits.

Watching the villagers move the *ogoh-ogoh* figures was nothing short of mesmerizing. The scene was a vivid display of collective energy and deep cultural significance. As the villagers hoisted the towering figures onto their shoulders, their movements were fluid yet deliberate, each step synchronized with the powerful rhythm of the drums that resonated through the air. The beat of the drums was steady and intense, like the pulse of the earth itself, reverberating through the ground and into our very bones. The sound seemed to carry the weight of centuries, echoing the devotion of generations who had participated in this sacred tradition.

The air was thick with a palpable energy—a mixture of excitement, reverence, and the anticipation of what was to come. The villagers moved in harmony, each one playing their part, some steadying the *ogoh-ogoh* while others swayed with the rhythm, guiding the figures through the streets with great care and respect. It wasn't just a parade; it was a sacred procession, one that bridged the earthly and the divine. The *ogoh-ogoh* themselves, with their fierce, painted faces and twisted limbs, seemed to come alive in the hands of their bearers, their heavy bodies swaying and shifting with every movement. It was as though the spirits they represented were stirring, preparing to be banished.

For a moment, it felt as though we had been transported back in time, into a world where the ancient rituals of Bali were still deeply woven into daily life. The scene unfolded like a living tapestry, where the present was intertwined with the past, and we were caught in the sweep of it all. As the villagers moved with purpose and devotion, it felt as though we were participating in something far larger than ourselves—something timeless, where each gesture, each offering, carried the weight of centuries of tradition. We weren't merely bystanders; we were part of a sacred rhythm, a shared experience that transcended time and place. The sight of these vibrant, larger-than-life figures parading through the streets, accompanied by the thunderous drumbeats and the chants of the villagers, left an indelible impression on our hearts—one that would stay with us long after the flames of the *ogoh-ogoh* had died down.

The crowd's energy was contagious, and we found ourselves cheering, clapping, and even joining in on the chanting. As the festival continued into the night, we felt a deep sense of gratitude for having the chance to experience something so meaningful. Bali's soul, its sense of community, and its respect for the sacred was alive in every smile, every chant, and every beat of the drum.

Now, let me tell you briefly, what the 'Ogoh Ogoh' festival is!

The 'Ogoh Ogoh' festival is one of Bali's most visually striking and culturally significant events, celebrated on the eve of 'Nyepi', the Balinese Day of Silence. Rooted deeply in Balinese Hinduism, the festival is both a spiritual ritual and a vivid artistic expression, designed to drive away negative energies and purify the island before the new year begins. The festival's central feature is the creation and procession of Ogoh Ogoh—towering, demon-like effigies symbolizing malevolent spirits. These statues are crafted by local communities using bamboo frames, papier-mâché, and cloth, and each statue is unique, often standing over several meters tall and painted in elaborate, menacing colours. With bulging eyes, fanged mouths, and outstretched arms, the Ogoh Ogoh figures are deliberately grotesque, meant to embody the forces of chaos and negativity that Balinese people believe can disrupt harmony.

The days leading up to the festival are filled with fervent activity, as artists, craftsmen, and community members come together to build and decorate these fearsome figures. As night falls on the day of the Ogoh Ogoh festival, villages across Bali come alive with drums, cymbals, and traditional music, setting an intense and electrifying atmosphere. Each Ogoh Ogoh is hoisted onto the shoulders of villagers, who parade it through the streets with a combination of chanting, dancing, and sudden, jerky movements, meant to frighten any lingering spirits. The statues are often twisted and spun during the procession, adding an almost surreal, chaotic energy to the ritual.

Once the procession reaches its climax, many communities symbolically destroy their Ogoh Ogoh by setting them ablaze, representing the purification of the island and the removal of malevolent influences. This final act releases the island from the influence of these evil spirits, setting the stage for 'Nyepi', the Day of Silence, when the entire island observes 24 hours of meditative quiet and reflection. The stark contrast between the boisterous 'Ogoh Ogoh' festival and the serenity of 'Nyepi' captures the balance of chaos and calm in Balinese spiritual life, making 'Ogoh Ogoh' not just a festival but a powerful cultural and religious experience.

That night, as we made our way back to our cozy bungalow, the feeling of tranquillity was overwhelming. The evening air, cool and crisp, wrapped around us like a soft embrace, and the faint rustle of leaves from the surrounding trees added to the serenity of the moment. Bali had unfolded before us like a beautifully crafted tapestry, each thread weaving together a perfect narrative of discovery and awe. The memories of the day lingered in our minds like the fading glow of the setting sun.

The misty morning at Sideman, where the clouds seemed to hover just inches above the earth, had set the stage for an unforgettable journey. We'd begun our day in a land of soft, ethereal light, enveloped by the mystical charm of Bali's hills and rice fields, and the quiet warmth of the village. From there, the calmness of Virgin Beach had been a pure escape—a rare slice of paradise where we had the vast expanse of the ocean almost entirely to ourselves. The water, so transparent and inviting, had seemed to wash away the remnants of our busy lives, allowing us to float in perfect contentment.

The quiet retreat of our Airbnb, tucked away amidst the hills, had offered a peaceful sanctuary, allowing us to sink into the natural beauty that surrounded us. The lush greenery, the gentle hillsides, and the distant waterfalls had all come together to create an atmosphere of utter calm, a place where time seemed to slow down and the world outside faded into the background.

And then, of course, there was the festival—the vibrant and powerful celebration of Bali's culture. The *ogoh-ogoh* procession, with its fiery passion and deep-rooted significance, had reminded us of the richness of the island's spiritual traditions. It had been a rare privilege to witness such a display of devotion, where every step, every beat of the drum, was infused with centuries of belief and reverence.

As we settled in for the night, our hearts were full, and our minds were at peace. Bali had shared its beauty, its spirit, and its soul with us in a way that felt personal and transformative. We had touched the essence of the island, and in doing so, it had left an indelible mark on us—a memory we would carry with us, a reminder of the magic that happens when nature, culture, and adventure converge in such a perfect harmony.

Chapter 8: The Sacred Silence of Nyepi

March 11, 2024

Our journey through Bali had been a vivid tapestry of rich experiences—an adventure painted with vibrant colours, awe-inspiring landscapes, and deep cultural encounters. From the misty mornings in Sideman to the serene beauty of Virgin Beach, every moment had felt like an exploration of both the island and our own senses. But as March 11th dawned, we were about to encounter something entirely different, something that would slow the pulse of the island and transform it into an entirely new experience. We were about to witness and partake in *Nyepi*, the Balinese Day of Silence.

Nyepi is a day that stands in stark contrast to the lively pace of daily life in Bali. Unlike any festival or celebration, we had encountered, this sacred day brings the entire island to a standstill. For 24 hours, everything is quiet, calm, and still, as the people of Bali dedicate themselves to spiritual renewal and reflection. The day is meant for cleansing—not just physically but spiritually—allowing the island to reset and rejuvenate, to purify itself for the year ahead.

As we prepared for Nyepi, it felt as though the very air had changed. Roads that were usually alive with the hum of scooters and the honking of taxis were now deserted. There were no vendors peddling their goods, no tourists strolling down the streets, and no hustle and bustle of everyday life. Even the busy beaches, usually filled with laughter and the sounds of waves crashing against the shore, seemed to hold their breath in anticipation. Bali, for once, became a place of quiet contemplation.

The temples, which had earlier in our journey echoed with prayers and offerings, were now still—almost sacredly silent—as if the very earth was pausing to listen to its own heartbeat. The energy of the island had shifted, and everything—from the bustling market stalls to the distant sounds of nature—fell into a harmonious stillness. It felt as if the island, its people, and its land were all synchronized in a collective breath, holding it just before the moment of renewal, like a deep, serene pause in the middle of a chaotic world.

For us, being in Bali on Nyepi was like stepping into a different realm. The sense of calm was palpable, and the day, though silent, carried an undercurrent of reverence and devotion. It was as though we had joined in a collective meditation, a practice that went beyond observation to immerse us in the spiritual heart of Bali itself. It was a rare and deeply humbling experience, one that allowed us to connect not just with the island's beauty but with its soul—a soul that rests not only in the vibrant festivals and the rich traditions of the Balinese people but also in the sacred silence that unites them all.

Nyepi is unlike anything we had ever experienced. It is not merely a holiday but a day for deep introspection and spiritual purification. On this day, the Balinese believe that evil spirits roam the island, and by keeping everything quiet and dark, they trick the spirits into believing the island is uninhabited. It’s a fascinating balance—a day of spiritual and physical reset. No one leaves their homes, and all lights are dimmed or turned off at night. Even Bali's international airport, typically bustling with tourists from around the world, closes entirely, a rare occurrence for any major airport globally. From sunrise to sunrise, Bali transforms into a world of introspective calm, an island collectively meditating.

We woke up to an unprecedented quiet. The usual sounds of chirping birds, distant motorbikes, or chatting neighbours were absent, replaced by an almost surreal stillness. The air felt heavy with reverence, and even the morning sunlight seemed softer, as if it too had taken on the island’s contemplative mood. For breakfast, we had a simple but delicious meal prepared by our Airbnb host: a crispy mahi-mahi fish fry, sandwiches with fresh vegetables and cheese, and a chilled glass of iced tea. Sitting by the ocean, we gazed out at the landscape, where even nature seemed to be holding its breath, wrapped in a sacred silence.

After breakfast, we decided to spend some time by the pool. As we slipped into the cool water, the sensation was calming and almost therapeutic, like the silence itself had a soothing effect. The pool’s surface was so still that every small ripple felt significant, and as we floated, it felt as though we were suspended in time. The water, the silence, and the muted colours of the sky created a surreal sense of peace, and for a moment, we felt entirely in tune with the spirit of Nyepi.

Later, we returned to our room and took an afternoon nap. Without the usual distractions of technology or noise, our minds were clearer, and we sank into a deep, restful sleep. By the time we woke up, the soft afternoon light had filled the room, casting a warm glow on the wooden walls. There was a peaceful energy in the air, a kind of tranquillity that we seldom experience in our usual fast-paced lives.

As the evening drew near, a sense of anticipation filled the air. The sky above was painted in soft hues of pink and orange, as the fading light of the day cast a tranquil glow over the surroundings. Our host, a gracious and kind woman who had made us feel so welcome from the moment we arrived, extended a heartfelt invitation to join her, her husband, and a few other guests for an early dinner. It was a gesture we welcomed eagerly, knowing that it would be a special opportunity to connect with others in a relaxed, homey setting.

At precisely 6 p.m., we made our way to the long wooden table that had been set outside, positioned under the gentle glow of candles that flickered in the evening breeze. The soft light created a warm, intimate atmosphere, casting gentle shadows and enhancing the feeling that we were gathered in a space suspended between day and night. The air was cool, fresh with the scents of the surrounding greenery, and the sounds of nature in the background—crickets chirping, the rustle of leaves—added to the serene ambiance. The atmosphere was peaceful, almost sacred, as if the quiet of the countryside had woven its way into the meal itself, and yet it was also filled with a friendly, welcoming energy.

Around the table, we were joined by a wonderfully diverse group of fellow travellers. A lively guest from Madrid, whose enthusiasm for life was infectious, regaled us with stories of his travels and experiences in Bali, his expressive gestures adding colour to each anecdote. A jovial man from Berlin, with a deep laugh and an easy manner, shared his love for local food and his adventures around the island. And then there was the charming couple from Ireland, their delightful Irish accents filling the air with warmth as they shared tales of their own homeland and their travels across the globe. Their laughter was contagious, and it felt as if the evening itself had wrapped us all in a blanket of shared camaraderie, bonding us through the simple joy of good food and great company.

As we ate, the conversation flowed naturally, punctuated by laughter and the clinking of glasses. Our host's husband, a quiet yet warm man, brought out plates of fresh, home-cooked dishes, each one more flavourful than the last. The flavours of Bali—spicy, aromatic, and rich—danced on our tongues as we savoured each bite. There was something deeply comforting about this shared experience: the feeling that we were part of a much larger tapestry, one that spanned countries, cultures, and continents, all coming together in this small, intimate moment.

The conversation flowed easily, a mix of laughter, curiosity, and the joy of meeting new friends from around the world. The man from Madrid shared stories of his travels across South America and Europe, his passion for food, and his love for Flamenco music, which he claimed was the most "soulful" music one could ever hear. The German guest, a quiet but warm presence, spoke about the different cultures he had encountered during his travels and marvelled at how Bali's spiritual energy was unlike any other place he had visited.

The Irish couple, humorous and socialized, recounted tales of the rugged landscapes of Ireland, the ancient castles, and the friendliness of their people. "You must come to Ireland!" the woman urged us, her eyes twinkling. "You'll fall in love with the greenery, and our hospitality is something we pride ourselves on." We laughed and nodded, feeling a new wanderlust spark inside us.

Our hosts, meanwhile, shared their journey of moving to Bali and the joys and challenges of building a life here. They spoke about how Nyepi had impacted them personally, describing it as a day of grounding and gratitude, a time when they feel truly connected to the land and its traditions. Listening to their stories made us appreciate how this island draws people from all over the world, each finding something unique here that resonates with their soul.

Dinner was a comforting meal of Balinese dishes, with a blend of local spices that left a lingering warmth. We laughed, shared stories, and appreciated the simplicity of this quiet evening, finding joy in the conversations and the sense of camaraderie that seemed to grow with each shared experience. Despite coming from different cultures, languages, and backgrounds, we all felt united in that moment, connected by our mutual love for travel and the spirit of exploration.

As the last bite of dinner was savoured and the final conversation wound down, we all stood up from the table, feeling the gentle pull of the evening's stillness. Our host's home, nestled in the heart of Sideman, seemed to hum with quiet energy, a peaceful reflection of the night around us. Stepping outside, we were immediately enveloped by the profound silence that had returned to the world. The noise of the day had been swallowed up, leaving only the natural sounds of the night: the rustling of the breeze through the palm trees, the occasional call of distant birds, and the soft murmur of the surrounding forest.

The sky above us had transformed into an inky black canvas, dotted with countless stars that shone with an intensity we had rarely witnessed before. Without the distractions of artificial lights, the stars seemed to fill the heavens, each one standing out in bold contrast against the velvety dark expanse. The vastness of the sky, untainted by city lights, took on an ethereal quality, as if the universe itself were within reach. We stood there in awe, silently taking it all in. The sheer number of stars above felt almost overwhelming, as if the heavens had opened just for this moment, allowing us to feel small and yet deeply connected to the vastness of the world.

In the stillness of that moment, time seemed to slow, and a deep sense of peace washed over us. There was something almost sacred about the night, as if we had tapped into a rhythm of life that had been beating for centuries, long before us and continuing long after we would leave. The stillness of Bali during Nyepi had brought us into harmony with the island's natural pulse, a reminder to pause, to breathe, and to reflect. We were not just visitors here; we felt like we were part of something ancient, timeless, and beautiful.

The absence of noise, the beauty of the sky, and the clarity of the moment made it feel as though we had stepped out of time, away from the rush of the modern world. The sense of solitude, combined with the connection to the earth, made everything seem more meaningful. There was a quiet invitation in the air—a call to reconnect with ourselves, with each other, and with nature. Bali, in all its harmony, had given us the space to reflect, to find peace in the present, and to be fully present in that still, star-filled night. We stood there, hand in hand, embracing the silence, feeling it seep into our souls, and knowing that this night, this moment, would stay with us forever.

That night, as we returned to our room and prepared to sleep, the gentle quiet of the island surrounded us once again. Nyepi had given us an unforgettable experience—a day of deep silence and stillness that left us feeling rejuvenated and grateful for this unique journey. In the quiet darkness, Bali had shown us a different kind of beauty, one that wasn't about landscapes or temples but about embracing the sacred calm within ourselves.

That night, as we returned to our room and began to settle in, the peaceful quiet of the island wrapped around us like a soft, comforting blanket. The air felt different now—calmer, more deliberate—as if the entire world had taken a collective breath and was holding it, just for a moment, in the deep embrace of the night. Outside, the gentle rustling of the trees in the breeze was the only sound that accompanied us as we slipped into our sanctuary, the soft glow of a single candle flickering beside us.

Nyepi had unfolded before us like a sacred ritual, a day of profound stillness that left its mark on our hearts in a way we hadn't expected. The absence of sound, the lack of movement—everything had come together to create an atmosphere of reverence, one that was both humbling and enlightening. We had experienced Bali in its rawest, purest form. There were no bustling crowds, no rushing from one place to the next. Instead, we had been invited to be present, to pause, to reflect. It was a day that challenged us to disconnect from the world and reconnect with ourselves, with the quiet rhythm of nature, and with the stillness within.

As we lay in the stillness of our room, a profound sense of gratitude filled us. We had come to Bali seeking adventure, beauty, and culture—but Nyepi had given us something even more precious: the space to slow down, to listen, and to feel the sacred quiet that had settled over the island. It was as though Bali had shown us a different kind of beauty—one that wasn't about the sweeping landscapes, the vibrant temples, or the endless horizons, but about the beauty found in silence, in stillness, and in the quiet moments of self-reflection.

The darkness outside felt rich with meaning, the kind of stillness that brings clarity and peace. There was a deep comfort in knowing that, for just a moment, the world had stopped, allowing us to reset, to breathe, and to appreciate the simple, sacred act of being. As we closed our eyes, we carried the calm of the day with us, the echoes of Nyepi lingering in our hearts, knowing that Bali had gifted us with a deeper connection to both the world and to ourselves.

Chapter 9: Nusa Penida – The Island of Turquoise Waters

March 12, 2024

The day after Nyepi, as dawn gently broke over Bali, the island seemed to inhale deeply, stretching out from its peaceful slumber. The stillness of the previous day slowly began to lift, replaced by the soft hum of life resuming its natural rhythm. The early morning light filtered through the trees, casting a serene glow across the landscape, as if the island itself was waking up with a quiet stretch, ready to embrace a new day. We could hear the distant sounds of roosters crowing, the rustle of leaves in the cool breeze, and the faint chatter of villagers beginning their morning routines.

With a deep sense of renewal from the stillness of Nyepi, we packed our bags, feeling lighter, more grounded, and filled with anticipation for the next chapter of our journey. The peaceful pause had given us a fresh perspective, a sense of clarity that made the world outside feel even more vibrant and alive. We were excited to continue our adventure, now with a deeper appreciation for the moments of quiet reflection that Bali had given us.

Our next destination was a place that had been on our minds since we'd arrived on the island—Nusa Penida. The name alone had intrigued us, with whispers of its jaw-dropping landscapes, crystal-clear waters, and untouched beauty. The island was known for its rugged cliffs, dramatic coastlines, and hidden beaches, a paradise that seemed almost too perfect to be real. We had heard tales of the island's natural wonders—the iconic Keling King Beach, the stunning Broken Beach, and the mesmerizing Angel's Billabong—and we couldn't wait to see it all for ourselves.

After a hearty breakfast and a final check of our bags, we set out for Sanur Port, where the ferry would take us across the Bali Sea to this elusive island. The port was calm in the early morning, with the soft waves lapping against the docks, the water shimmering under the first rays of sunlight. The ferry was waiting, ready to whisk us away on an adventure that promised to be nothing short of extraordinary. As we boarded, the gentle hum of the engine signalled the beginning of our journey, and we sat back, taking one last look at Bali's shores as the boat began to pull away.

The cool breeze on the deck, the sound of the water beneath us, and the excitement building inside us made the short journey feel like the start of something special. We could already imagine the pristine beauty of Nusa Penida, the crystal-clear waters, the dramatic cliffs, and the peaceful escape it promised. It was a new chapter in our Bali adventure, and we were ready to embrace whatever magic awaited us on the other side of the sea.

Our ferry, named Caspla, was a speedboat that promised not just a quick journey but an exhilarating one. As we climbed on board and settled into our seats, we felt the anticipation building. Soon, the engines roared to life, and the boat surged forward, cutting through the waves with a rush of energy. The sea was stunningly blue, and each wave glistened under the morning sun. We felt the salty spray on our faces, and with every bounce over the waves, we felt the thrill of adventure. The half-hour journey to Nusa Penida flew by as we marvelled at the ever-deepening shades of blue around us. The water had an almost surreal quality to it, unlike anything we'd seen before.

As the ferry gently docked at Nusa Penida's port, the anticipation in the air was palpable. We stepped off the boat, the warm island breeze instantly wrapping around us, carrying with it the faint scent of saltwater and tropical flowers. The moment our feet touched the soft, golden sand, a wave of awe washed over us. The surroundings were nothing short of magical—Nusa Penida was like a dream brought to life.

The water before us was an ethereal shade of turquoise, so vibrant and crystal-clear that it almost seemed unreal, like something plucked straight from a postcard. It shimmered in the sunlight, the waves gently lapping against the shore in a rhythm that felt soothing, almost meditative. We stood there for a moment, eyes wide, taking in the view—a vast expanse of ocean stretching endlessly to meet the horizon, framed by rugged cliffs and lush greenery. It was the kind of beauty that took your breath away, as if the island was holding its secrets close, waiting for us to uncover them one by one.

We couldn't help but feel a profound sense of wonder as we soaked in the stunning scenery. It was our first time experiencing such an untouched, raw natural beauty, and it felt like we had stepped into a hidden paradise. Every corner of Nusa Penida seemed to have something new to reveal, from the sparkling waters to the towering cliffs, each more breathtaking than the last.

But as much as we wanted to remain lost in the beauty of the port, there was no time to waste. Our adventure had just begun. We quickly rented a scooter, excited by the thought of exploring the island at our own pace. The freedom of the open road beckoned, and we were eager to see what lay ahead. We dropped off our bags at our cozy Airbnb, a small haven nestled among the island's natural beauty, and set off with the wind in our hair and hearts full of excitement.

The road stretched before us, winding through the island's verdant landscapes, dotted with vibrant flowers, towering palm trees, and the occasional glimpse of the sparkling coastline. Every turn seemed to lead us deeper into a world of wonder, with hidden beaches, dramatic cliffs, and ancient temples just waiting to be discovered. Nusa Penida had a wild, untamed beauty that felt like an explorer's dream, and we were ready to immerse ourselves fully in its magic.

Our first destination on Nusa Penida was the legendary Kelingking Beach, also known as Klingking Beach—a place we'd heard so much about, and now we were finally going to experience it for ourselves. The journey to reach this iconic spot was an adventure in itself, taking us through the heart of Nusa Penida's rugged terrain. We wound our way through dense, vibrant greenery, the scent of tropical plants filling the air. Towering cliffs loomed above us, their jagged edges meeting the soft blue sky, while the distant sound of the ocean crashing against the rocks teased our ears.

The road was far from smooth—bumpy and uneven, with occasional dips and sharp curves that kept us on our toes as we navigated the path. But the challenges only added to the thrill of the ride, and with each twist and turn, our excitement built. We could feel the anticipation in the air, knowing that what awaited us at the end of this journey would be nothing short of extraordinary.

Finally, we arrived at the viewpoint, and the sight that greeted us was beyond anything we had imagined. Standing at the edge of the cliff, we were hit with a wave of awe. Before us, the land unfolded like a living masterpiece, a sweeping panorama of dramatic cliffs plunging into the turquoise sea. The most striking feature was the iconic T-Rex-shaped rock formation, its enormous curves stretching out into the ocean as if some ancient creature had once rested here, now frozen in time. It was a surreal sight—so perfectly formed that it looked almost otherworldly.

As we gazed down, the ocean below was a sight to behold—waves crashing with powerful force against the base of the cliff, sending white foam splashing into the air. Nestled in the curve of the rock, Kelingking Beach lay like a hidden gem, a pristine strip of powdery white sand bordered by the most vibrant shades of blue we had ever seen. The water sparkled in the sunlight, shifting from a deep sapphire at the edges to a lighter, almost translucent turquoise closer to shore. The beach was secluded, serene, and untouched, as if it existed in its own secret world, far from the reach of the crowds.

We stood there for what felt like an eternity, taking it all in, utterly speechless. The sheer beauty of the scene—its raw, unspoiled nature—left us with a sense of wonder we could hardly put into words. It was the kind of place that felt like a dream, a reminder of just how extraordinary the natural world can be. We could have stayed there forever, entranced by the beauty that lay before us, but the allure of exploring this stunning island was too strong to resist.

The view before us was simply surreal, unlike anything we had ever seen. Time seemed to slow as we stood there, side by side, taking it all in. The landscape stretched out in front of us, vast and unspoiled, with the crystal-clear waters and dramatic cliffs blending together in a scene so perfect it could have been plucked from a dream. We held hands in silence, not wanting to break the spell, as if by speaking we might disturb the incredible equanimity that surrounded us. Every detail—the shimmering ocean, the jagged rocks, the way the light danced across the water—was etched into our minds, and we knew we would carry this moment with us forever.

There was an undeniable magic in the air, something deeply ancient and sacred, as if we had stumbled upon a place that time had forgotten. It was as though we were standing at the edge of the earth, gazing upon a world untouched by the hustle and bustle of modern life. The landscape seemed to breathe with a kind of quiet power, and we felt a deep connection to it—a humbling reminder of the raw beauty and majesty of nature.

We took a few photos, of course, but honestly, they didn't do the scene justice. No picture could fully capture the awe we felt standing there in person. We simply stood, allowing ourselves to be enveloped by the wonder of it all. The world felt vast, yet we were so small in comparison to the grandeur of the cliffs and the ocean, and in that moment, it was enough to just be present.

Around us, other travellers stood in similar reverence, their faces illuminated with the same wide-eyed wonder we felt. We exchanged smiles and knowing glances with a group of fellow explorers from Australia, who were just as entranced by the view as we were. One of them, a man with a look of pure disbelief on his face, muttered, "This place is unreal," shaking his head in amazement. We all nodded in agreement, as words felt entirely inadequate to describe what we were witnessing. It was the kind of moment that defied explanation, and the only way to truly understand it was to experience it for yourself. We were all sharing in the same awe, standing together in the presence of something truly extraordinary.

Reluctantly, we tore ourselves away from the breathtaking view at Kelingking Beach, the scene still etched in our minds as we made our way toward the next destination: Angel's Billabong. As we rode along the winding roads, the anticipation grew, but nothing could have quite prepared us for the otherworldly beauty that awaited us.

Angel's Billabong felt like stepping into a hidden paradise, where nature's artistry was on full display. The rock formations here were nothing short of mesmerizing—smooth, jagged cliffs that surrounded a natural infinity pool, the water within a stunning blend of crystal-clear blues and vibrant greens. It was as though the earth itself had sculpted this serene oasis, a peaceful retreat carved into the landscape. We found a spot on the edge of the rocks, the sun warm on our faces as we dipped our feet into the cool water. The gentle lapping of the waves created a soothing rhythm, and every so often, a wave would splash over the rocks, refreshing us with its cool embrace. Sitting there, with the vast ocean stretching out before us, it felt as if we were perched at the edge of the world, disconnected from everything else, with only the beauty of nature to keep us company.

We could have stayed there forever, but the adventure called us forward. Just a short walk away, we arrived at Broken Beach, another stunning wonder of nature. The cliffs here were dramatic, rising high above a natural archway carved into the stone by centuries of ocean waves. Below, the sea roared through the arch, sending powerful waves crashing against the rocks and creating a thunderous sound that reverberated through the air. The contrast between the emerald green water and the rugged rock formations was striking, and the sight of the ocean rushing through the archway was a reminder of the wild power of nature. The atmosphere was one of raw, untamed beauty—a blend of serenity and strength that left us in awe. The sound of the crashing waves and the sight of the sparkling water beneath us created a sense of deep connection to the earth, as if we were witnessing nature's most primal forces at work. In that moment, we felt a profound sense of peace and wonder, reminded of the immense beauty and power of the world around us.

As the afternoon stretched on, we made our way to Crystal Bay Beach, the perfect place to unwind after a day filled with exploration. The moment we arrived, we were enveloped by the peaceful atmosphere of this hidden cove. Crystal Bay was a serene retreat, a tucked-away paradise surrounded by swaying palm trees and soft, golden sands that seemed to invite us to relax.

We found a quiet spot near the water's edge, spread out a towel, and lay back, feeling the soothing warmth of the sun sinking deep into our skin. The air was warm, yet the breeze kept things comfortably cool, carrying with it the salty scent of the sea. The sound of the waves gently lapping against the shore became the soundtrack to our afternoon, their rhythmic ebb and flow gradually lulling us into a state of pure bliss. Time seemed to slow down as we relaxed into the moment, completely at peace in this tranquil corner of the world.

As the hours passed, the sky began to transform. The golden afternoon light shifted into warm hues of pink and orange, casting a soft, glowing light over the bay. The water, once a vibrant turquoise, turned into shades of deep coral and lavender as the sun sank lower toward the horizon. We sat up for a better view, watching in awe as the sky melted into a stunning canvas of colour. The waves reflected the sky's changing shades, creating a harmonious dance of light and water. The atmosphere was peaceful, almost magical, as if the world itself was holding its breath for that perfect, fleeting moment.

In the silence of the beach, we shared a glance, no words needed. There was a deep sense of gratitude in the air, a quiet acknowledgment of the beauty of this moment and the journey that had brought us here. As the sun finally dipped below the horizon, leaving only a trace of its glow in the sky, we felt content, knowing that this was one of those moments we would carry with us forever. Crystal Bay had gifted us not just a stunning sunset, but a moment of pure serenity, reminding us to slow down, breathe, and soak in the simple yet profound beauty of the world.

As the final rays of sunlight dipped below the horizon, we slowly made our way back to our Airbnb, our hearts overflowing with the beauty and wonder of the day. The memories of Kelingking Beach, Angel's Billabong, and Crystal Bay still lingered in our minds, vivid and serene. But despite the peaceful contentment that came with such a perfect day, the evening held one more treat for us. After so many days of diving into Bali's unique and delicious flavours, we found ourselves craving the comforting familiarity of home. As we strolled through the village, we spotted an Indian restaurant named 'Bollywood Indian Cuisine' tucked away on a quiet corner, its inviting aroma wafting through the air and stirring our appetites.

It was a spontaneous decision, but one that felt just right. The thought of sinking our teeth into familiar spices and flavours, after all the exotic dishes we had tried, felt like a warm embrace. We entered the cozy, softly lit space, where the sounds of clinking dishes and quiet chatter filled the air, and the scent of cumin, turmeric, and garlic greeted us like an old friend. Our eyes immediately landed on the restaurant's specialty, and we exchanged excited glances. The biryani, with its rich, fragrant rice and tender pieces of meat, was a dish we couldn't resist.

As the food arrived at our table, the vibrant colors and intoxicating aromas made our mouths water. Each bite was a comforting blend of spices that transported us back to memories of home, while still maintaining its own delicious twist. We savoured every spoonful, enjoying the contrast between the familiar warmth of the spices and the exotic surroundings of Bali. The meal felt like the perfect way to close out an unforgettable day—a reminder that even in the farthest corners of the world, there's always room for a little taste of home. The aroma hit us as soon as we stepped inside, filling us with an instant feeling of nostalgia. We ordered the biryani and dug in with unabashed enthusiasm, savouring each bite of the fragrant, spice-infused rice. It was comforting and delicious, a reminder of home in the midst of our island adventure. By the time we left the restaurant, our stomachs were happily full, and we were ready to call it a night, feeling completely content and deeply fulfilled by the day.

That night, as we nestled into the soft embrace of our bed, the magic of Nusa Penida's landscapes danced in our minds, refusing to let go. The memories were vivid—like snapshots frozen in time. The towering cliffs of Kelingking Beach, their jagged edges framed against a boundless ocean, seemed to pulse with the energy of the island, while the serene, crystal-clear waters of Angel's Billabong glistened like liquid jade, inviting us to dive deeper into nature's beauty. The tranquil calm of Crystal Bay, where the gentle lapping of waves seemed to whisper peace into our souls, and the mesmerizing colours of the sunset reflecting on the water, added a sense of quiet joy to our hearts. Even the simple yet profound pleasure of the biryani at dinner, a comforting taste of home in an unfamiliar place, wove its way into the fabric of the day.

Lying in the cool, quiet darkness, the events of the day seemed to unfold like a beautiful story we never wanted to end. Each place we visited felt like a chapter in a book we'd always want to revisit, each memory imprinted upon our hearts with a sense of awe and fulfilment. There was something profoundly special about how this day had blended adventure and serenity—how the wild beauty of the island had stirred our spirits, while the simple comforts had grounded us. It was a day that had offered us a perfect balance of awe, joy, and reflection, a reminder that travel isn't just about the places you visit, but the moments that leave an imprint on your soul.

As we drifted off to sleep, a sense of contentment settled over us. We knew that this day would stay with us for years to come, a cherished chapter in our journey, a reminder of the wonders of the world, and of the quiet moments that make it all feel so deeply meaningful.

\Chapter 10: Diamond Dreams and Farewell to Penida

March 13, 2024

On Nusa Penida, where the oceans gleam,

In hues of turquoise, a vivid dream.

Cliffs draped in green, the waves' soft song,

A paradise where hearts belong.

\- *Krittika*

With the sun casting its golden light over Nusa Penida, we woke to a warm, misty morning that seemed to hold the promise of new discoveries. The air carried a crisp freshness, and as we stepped out of our cozy Airbnb, the island seemed to stretch and yawn awake alongside us. By 7 a.m., we were on our rented scooter, its familiar hum blending with the gentle sounds of birds and rustling leaves. There was a palpable sense of excitement as we set off for our destination of the day: *Diamond Beach*. This was a place we had seen in countless pictures, each one more breathtaking than the last, and now, it was our turn to witness its beauty firsthand.

The journey itself was an adventure, the kind that etches itself into your memory. As we rode along the cliffside roads, the sheer grandeur of the landscape unfolded with every turn. Narrow paths, bordered by lush green vegetation, curved gracefully along the edges of steep cliffs that seemed to tumble into the ocean below. Palm trees swayed gently in the morning breeze, their emerald fronds glistening with dew. The Balinese Sea, a mesmerizing spectrum of blues, stretched endlessly beside us, shimmering like liquid sapphire under the rising sun.

Each bend in the road revealed a new scene more stunning than the last, as if nature had designed this route to showcase its finest work. The contrast of the vibrant greenery against the vast expanse of the ocean was hypnotic, and we found ourselves pausing now and then just to take it all in. It felt as though we were gliding through a living postcard, with the beauty of Nusa Penida unfolding before us in real time. The thrill of the open road, the anticipation of our destination, and the quiet joy of being surrounded by such raw, unspoiled beauty made the morning ride feel like a perfect prelude to the wonders that awaited us at Diamond Beach.

As we rode through the hills, the morning breeze was gentle but carried a certain energy, heightening the excitement in the air. The sheer cliffs, covered in dense foliage, dropped dramatically into the deep turquoise waters below. We'd grown somewhat used to Bali's natural beauty by now, but the landscape of Nusa Penida was strikingly unique, marked by craggy peaks and rolling hills that cascaded into the ocean in shades of emerald and sapphire. It was impossible not to feel completely alive, with each twist and turn of the road leading us further into nature's embrace.

Finally, we arrived at Diamond Beach, a name that seemed to promise something extraordinary—and it delivered beyond anything we had imagined. Climbing off the scooter, we followed a winding trail carved into the rugged cliffs, the path offering tantalizing glimpses of the beauty that awaited us below. As we descended, the view before us unfurled like a masterpiece hidden until the perfect moment.

The beach lived up to its name in every way. Jagged limestone rocks jutted dramatically out of the crystal-clear turquoise waters, their sharp edges glinting in the sunlight like scattered diamonds strewn across the sea. These natural formations stood proud and striking, resembling precious stones placed with deliberate care, their beauty intensified by the way the waves gently lapped against their bases. The cliffs surrounding the beach were a spectacle in themselves, their rocky faces layered with shades of white and grey, dotted with patches of vibrant green vegetation that clung tenaciously to their surfaces.

As our eyes travelled downward, the pale, powdery sand came into view, a pristine shoreline that looked untouched and impossibly inviting. The gentle waves, shimmering under the golden rays of the sun, rolled onto the beach in a soft, rhythmic dance, their foam sparkling as if sprinkled with stardust. The scene felt almost surreal, as though it belonged to another world—one that had been crafted with the precision and artistry of a jeweller creating their finest work.

We paused for a moment on the trail, speechless and captivated by the sheer majesty of Diamond Beach. It was a vision of nature at its most exquisite, a perfect harmony of rugged cliffs, crystalline waters, and sunlit sands that seemed to whisper secrets of the earth's ancient past. The allure of the beach was irresistible, drawing us forward with the promise of tranquillity and wonder, and we couldn't wait to step onto its shores and immerse ourselves in its magic.

We carefully made our way down the steps carved into the cliffside, each one taking us closer to the glistening shoreline. When we finally reached the bottom, the sight of the beach was mesmerizing—soft sand, bright blue waters, and towering stone formations that seemed to guard the cove. The beach felt untouched, as if hidden away just for us. We removed our shoes, letting the fine sand cover our feet, feeling the cool ocean breeze on our faces. The waves lapped at the shore, playful yet powerful, and we wandered along the coastline, pausing every few steps to take in the surreal landscape.

A few other travellers were scattered across the beach, their figures small against the grandeur of the landscape. Some lounged peacefully on the powdery sand, soaking in the warmth of the sun, while others wandered along the shoreline, their expressions reflecting the same sense of awe that mirrored our own. The atmosphere was serene, filled only with the gentle sound of waves meeting the shore and the occasional laughter or exclamation of wonder.

As we strolled along, our gaze met that of a young couple from Canada. Their friendly smiles invited conversation, and soon we were chatting like old friends. They shared tales of their adventures, recounting their journeys through Southeast Asia, while we described the treasures we had discovered in Bali and Nusa Penida. The conversation flowed easily, punctuated by laughter and shared amazement at the beauty surrounding us. It was a meeting of kindred spirits, all brought together by the universal language of nature's artistry.

Standing there on Diamond Beach, thousands of miles from home, it felt surreal to connect so deeply with strangers. The towering limestone formations, the turquoise waves, and the sunlit sands served as a breathtaking backdrop to our shared stories. In that moment, we weren't just travellers passing through; we were part of a global community of explorers, united by our love for the world's wonders. It was a reminder of how travel has the power to create bonds that transcend borders, leaving us with not just memories of places, but also of the people we meet along the way.

Time seemed to dissolve as we immersed ourselves in the beauty of Diamond Beach. Each step along the soft, powdery sand felt like a discovery—tiny seashells glinting in the sunlight, intricate patterns etched by retreating waves, and the gentle foam that danced along the shoreline before disappearing into the sea. The hours flowed seamlessly, marked not by a clock but by moments of pure joy and awe.

We took countless photos, attempting to capture even a fraction of the magic that surrounded us. The camera's lens tried to frame the brilliance of the waves as they sparkled under the sun, each ripple catching the light like liquid diamonds. Between shots, our laughter echoed against the towering limestone cliffs, a melody carried away by the breeze.

The sound of the sea was mesmerizing, a rhythmic symphony that seemed to resonate with the pulse of the earth. As the waves crashed against the jagged rock formations, they created a harmonious blend of power and serenity—a reminder of nature's raw strength and delicate artistry. We paused often, just to take it all in, letting the vast expanse of blue before us draw our gaze into its infinite embrace.

Every detail felt like a gift, from the sun's warmth on our skin to the gentle wind that teased our hair. Standing on that beach, we couldn't help but marvel at our fortune—to witness a place so untouched, so perfect, that it felt as though it existed in its own sacred realm. In those hours, Diamond Beach wasn't just a destination; it was an experience that left us humbled and deeply grateful for the wonders of the world.

As the afternoon sun climbed higher, we decided to make our way back up the cliffside path, casting one last, longing glance at Diamond Beach. Back on our scooter, we spent the rest of the afternoon exploring more of Nusa Penida, meandering through the hilly paths and soaking up every view of the ocean and cliffs that we could. Riding through the island, we felt a deep connection to this place—a sense of freedom, adventure, and peace that's hard to capture in words.

Eventually, the time came to bid farewell to Nusa Penida. We returned the scooter, collected our bags, and headed back to the port. The Penida Express ferry was waiting to take us back to Bali, and as we boarded, we felt a bittersweet twinge of nostalgia, already missing the island we had come to love. The ferry ride back was calm, and we sat side by side, watching the island grow smaller on the horizon, feeling grateful for every memory we'd made there.

By the time we returned to Bali, the horizon was painted in hues of deep orange and purple, with the last light of day slowly fading into night. The city lights began to shimmer like scattered jewels in the warm evening air, casting a soft, golden glow over the bustling streets of Sanur. There was a sense of serenity mixed with a bittersweet realization—this was our final night on the island, a place that had given us memories to cherish for a lifetime.

Wanting to make the evening special, we decided to treat ourselves to a candlelit dinner at an Indian restaurant we had discovered earlier. As we stepped inside, the restaurant welcomed us with its intimate charm. The flickering glow of candles reflected off the polished wooden tables, creating a cozy and romantic ambiance. The air was filled with the unmistakable aroma of familiar spices—

cardamom, cumin, and saffron—a sensory reminder of home that instantly brought comfort and warmth to our hearts.

The decor was understated yet elegant, with colourful drapes and traditional motifs adorning the walls. Soft, melodic strains of Indian classical music played in the background, weaving a tapestry of nostalgia and serenity. We chose a quiet corner table and settled in, the soft hum of conversation and clinking cutlery around us blending into the gentle rhythm of the evening.

As we scanned the menu, memories of our travels mingled with the anticipation of a hearty meal. The dishes we ordered arrived promptly, served with a warmth that mirrored the hospitality of the staff. Each bite was a celebration of flavours—rich, spicy, and deeply satisfying. It felt like a fitting conclusion to our journey, a connection to our roots even as we sat in the heart of Bali, thousands of miles from home.

The evening unfolded with laughter, shared stories, and a quiet reflection of everything we had experienced over the past days. It was a moment to savour, not just the food but the culmination of a journey that had been equal parts adventure, discovery, and peace. As we clinked our glasses in a final toast, the candlelight danced between us, illuminating not just our faces but the gratitude and joy in our hearts.

The staff greeted us warmly, guiding us to a small, private table, and we ordered our favourite dishes. The flavours were rich, comforting, and each bite was like a taste of home, blending perfectly with the sense of nostalgia and gratitude we felt. We laughed, reminisced about our days on the island, and talked about the many beautiful moments that had filled our journey. As we enjoyed the meal, we could hear the distant hum of the city, but inside the restaurant, time seemed to slow down, allowing us to savour each moment.

After dinner, we stepped out into the warm evening air of Sanur, the streets buzzing with life and energy. The vibrant hum of the town embraced us as we strolled hand-in-hand, letting the rhythm of the nightlife guide our steps. Lanterns and fairy lights strung between buildings cast a soft, golden glow over the bustling sidewalks, where travellers from all corners of the world mingled with locals. The atmosphere was alive with the joyous sounds of laughter, music, and the gentle murmur of ocean waves in the distance.

Street performers captured small crowds with their talents—guitarists strumming soulful melodies, dancers moving gracefully to traditional Balinese rhythms, and even a magician entertaining an awestruck group of children. Vendors lined the streets, their stalls brimming with colourful trinkets, handcrafted jewellery, and vibrant batik fabrics. The aroma of roasted peanuts and grilled satay wafted through the air, mingling with the faint scent of salt carried on the breeze.

We meandered through the lively scene, stopping occasionally to admire the artistry of a handcrafted souvenir or exchange a few words with a friendly vendor. The conversations were brief but warm, reflecting the island's signature hospitality that had made us feel so welcome. At times, we simply paused to soak in the view—children chasing each other with glowing balloons, couples laughing over drinks at open-air cafes, and groups of friends clinking glasses in celebration.

As we walked further, the street noise softened, and the town's vibrancy gave way to a quieter charm. The twinkling lights overhead mirrored the stars above, creating a dreamy atmosphere. Hand-in-hand, we reflected on the journey we had just shared, the adventures, the landscapes, and the people who had made Bali unforgettable. The world around us felt both intimate and vast, as if this small corner of Bali held infinite stories waiting to unfold.

We strolled along the beachside promenade, where the gentle lapping of the waves accompanied us. The moonlight shimmered on the water, and the night's coolness felt soothing against our skin. It was a perfect way to say goodbye to Bali—a leisurely walk filled with the vibrancy, beauty, and magic of the island, ensuring that its spirit would remain with us long after we'd gone.

Finally, as the night deepened and the energy of the day began to settle, we made our way back to our hotel. The streets, now quieter, seemed to echo with the faint remnants of laughter and music, the perfect lullaby for a day so vibrant and full. Our bodies were weary but our spirits soared, buoyed by the countless memories we had gathered like precious treasures throughout the day.

Diamond Beach's surreal beauty lingered in our thoughts—the pristine sands, the towering limestone formations, and the infinite blue of the ocean. The thrill of riding the quiet roads of Nusa Penida, with the wind on our faces and the promise of discovery around every turn, replayed like a vivid dream. The warmth of the candlelit dinner, with its comforting flavours and the soft glow of companionship, wrapped around us like a gentle embrace. And finally, the lively streets of Kuta, with their blend of chaos and charm, seemed to hum faintly in our memories, like an island's heartbeat we had briefly been part of.

As we slipped into the cool comfort of our bed, the events of the day swirled together, forming a tapestry of adventure, serenity, and joy. We lay there for a while, letting the weight of gratitude settle over us—grateful for the stunning landscapes we had seen, for the kindred spirits we had met, for the cultural richness of Bali, and for the simple, profound gift of being able to travel and experience it all.

Soon, the exhaustion of the day gave way to the pull of sleep. Our minds, still brimming with the sights and sounds of paradise, began to quiet. Drifting off, we knew this was more than just a journey; it was a chapter of our lives that would forever remind us of the world's endless beauty and the importance of embracing it with open hearts.

Chapter 11: Farewell, Bali

March 14, 2024

As the gentle morning light filtered through the curtains, painting the room in soft hues of gold and lavender, a quiet melancholy settled over us. It was the kind of light that made everything seem suspended in time, and for a moment, we allowed ourselves to bask in its warmth, unwilling to disturb the serenity. But as we glanced at our suitcases, half-packed and waiting by the door, the bittersweet truth began to dawn on us—our time in Bali had reached its end.

Every corner of this island had left its mark on us, each moment becoming a piece of a mosaic that felt too precious to leave behind. The warm smiles of the Balinese people, their gentle "Selamat pagi" greetings, and the way they welcomed us into their culture with open arms had created a connection that went far deeper than we had anticipated. The landscapes, too, had cast their spell on us—emerald rice terraces, misty mountaintops, crystal-clear beaches, and hidden waterfalls that seemed to whisper secrets of the earth.

As we packed the last of our belongings, each item seemed to carry a memory. Sand stuck to the soles of our shoes, reminding us of our walks along Diamond Beach. The aroma of spices clinging faintly to our clothes took us back to candlelit dinners and bustling street markets. Even the scooter key we reluctantly handed back seemed imbued with the spirit of winding cliffside roads and the thrill of adventure.

This had been more than a vacation; it had been an awakening. Bali had shown us a rhythm of life that was both slower and richer, where beauty was not just seen but felt, and where every moment seemed to hum with a quiet sense of purpose. As we zipped up the last bag, a profound gratitude filled our hearts. This wasn't a goodbye; it was a promise—a promise to carry the lessons of this island with us and to one day return to its warm embrace.

We quietly closed the door to our room, taking one last look around before heading out. The streets were calm, still waking up to the first glimmers of sunlight. As we rode to the airport, passing the familiar sights of Bali one last time, we couldn't help but feel a pang of sadness. With every bend in the road, we whispered silent goodbyes to the places that had meant so much to us.

At the airport, the reality of parting settled heavily in our hearts. The vibrant energy of the terminal contrasted sharply with the quiet ache of leaving behind a place that had become so dear to us. We moved slowly through the bustling crowd, trying to savour every moment of these final hours in this land of unparalleled beauty. Every glance around the terminal seemed to carry the essence of Bali—the soft hum of conversation in multiple languages, the scent of incense wafting faintly from a nearby shop, and the cheerful smiles of locals bidding farewell to travellers like us.

We wandered through the souvenir shops; our steps deliberate as we searched for tokens that would carry the soul of the island back with us. A small statue from Uluwatu caught our eye, its craftsmanship embodying the skill and reverence of the Balinese people. Nearby, intricately carved wooden figures seemed to tell their own stories, each one as unique as the moments we had lived here. We ran our fingers over vibrant textiles, their patterns a kaleidoscope of colour and tradition, and chose a few to remind us of the cultural richness we had encountered. Finally, we couldn't resist picking up jars of the fragrant Balinese coffee, its earthy aroma evoking memories of misty mornings on the verandah, watching the sun rise over the hills.

Each item we selected felt like more than just a souvenir; it was a tangible piece of the island, a connection to the sights, sounds, and emotions that had shaped our journey. As we packed them into our carry-on bags, we couldn't help but smile, knowing these treasures would keep Bali close, no matter how far we travelled. With every step toward the departure gate, the weight of leaving grew heavier, but so too did our gratitude for all we had experienced. These mementos were more than keepsakes—they were promises to ourselves to hold onto the magic of Bali long after we said goodbye.

Finally, as we waited for boarding, we found a quiet corner away from the bustling crowd, a small refuge amidst the commotion of the airport. Around us, travellers hurried to and from, their suitcases rolling noisily across the polished floors, their voices blending into a low, constant hum. Yet in our little space, time seemed to slow, giving us a chance to reflect on the incredible journey that was now drawing to a close.

We sat in comfortable silence, the weight of the moment settling over us. The scenes from our adventure played in our minds like a vivid montage—the golden hues of early mornings spent watching the sun rise over ancient temples, the tranquil beauty of sunsets casting a warm glow over rice fields, and the echo of waves crashing against the cliffs as we stood in awe of nature's grandeur. Every memory felt alive, as though we could still feel the cool mist of waterfalls on our skin, hear the distant chants from temple ceremonies, and taste the exotic spices that had delighted our palates.

We smiled at the thought of the people we'd met along the way, their faces flashing through our minds like snapshots in an album. Strangers turned into friends over shared laughter, heartfelt conversations, and the universal language of wonder. The Canadian couple at Diamond Beach, the Irish pair with their charming accents, and Ketut, whose stories about her village festival had brought us closer to Bali's rich culture—all had added layers of depth to our experience.

It felt surreal to think that just days ago, we had been trekking volcanoes under starlit skies, floating in crystal-clear waters, and walking along beaches so pristine they seemed almost otherworldly. Those moments, which had once felt infinite, now lingered as bittersweet memories, already tinged with nostalgia. In this quiet pause, surrounded by the transitory energy of an airport, we realized how profoundly this journey had touched us. Bali was no longer just a destination—it had become a part of us, woven into our hearts and minds in a way that would remain long after we returned home.

Our flight was called, and we reluctantly walked toward the gate. As the plane ascended, the island faded beneath us, the verdant mountains and coastlines shrinking into a patchwork of green and blue. We watched until Bali disappeared entirely, holding on to the last glimpse of the island, our hearts heavy yet full.

The next leg of our journey took us to Kuala Lumpur, where we had a six-hour layover. Though the vibrant city of Kuala Lumpur stretched just beyond the airport walls, we were in a pensive mood, still processing our farewell to Bali. We found a quiet lounge, settling down with coffee as we shared our reflections on the journey. It was amazing how much we had experienced, and how deeply those experiences had impacted us. We talked about the people we'd met, the laughter shared, the breathtaking sights, and the serenity that seemed to permeate every corner of the island.

In that quiet moment, as we sat in the soft glow of the airport terminal, the weight of our journey began to settle in deeper. It wasn't just the stunning landscapes of Bali, or the incredible places we'd seen that made this trip unforgettable. It was the way we had shared it all together, side by side, discovering new experiences, facing challenges, and embracing each moment with open hearts. The laughter we shared over dinner, the quiet moments as we watched sunsets together, the joy of navigating unknown paths—these were the threads that had woven us closer, binding us through the adventure.

Every day had felt like a new chapter in a story that was as much about the places we visited as it was about the connection between us. There was something uniquely profound in the way we had explored Bali together—how the island's beauty had sparked conversations, how the rituals and traditions we witnessed had deepened our understanding of one another and the world around us. Whether we were climbing up to a temple or lounging by the ocean, there had been a subtle magic in each shared glance, each spontaneous laugh, each moment of awe that we experienced together.

We realized that through this journey, we had discovered not just the wonders of Bali, but also the strength of our bond. The shared wonder of seeing a breathtaking sunrise, the thrill of trying new foods, or the contentment of sitting in silence together, watching the waves, had cemented our connection in a way that would stay with us long after the trip was over. Bali had given us the gift of truly being present with each other, of relishing the fleeting moments, and of embracing the beauty of life in all its forms.

The journey had been more than just a series of destinations—it had been an ongoing celebration of life itself. A reminder that the true richness of any adventure lies not just in the places we go, but in the connections, we make, the memories we create, and the love that grows stronger with every step we take together. In that quiet moment, we knew this journey had changed us, had brought us closer, and that these memories, shared between us, would last a lifetime.

As the hours passed, we reminisced about every temple, beach, and street that had left an imprint on our souls. Soon enough, our boarding call came, and we returned to our seats for the final flight home. Watching the world pass by through the window, we knew that Bali had left an indelible mark on us, shaping us in ways that we would cherish for years to come.

As the plane descended toward Kolkata, the view of the sprawling city and its familiar landmarks began to stir a sense of both nostalgia and comfort. The hum of the plane gradually softened, and we looked out the window, feeling a wave of warmth as the landscape below unfolded before us. It was strange yet beautiful to be returning to a place we called home after days spent in the magic of Bali. But in that moment, Bali, with all its vibrant colours, stunning vistas, and cultural richness, still felt close to our hearts, as if it had woven itself into the fabric of who we were.

Despite the excitement of returning, there was a quiet sadness as we thought about leaving the island behind. Bali had touched us in a way few places could—its peaceful mornings, the warmth of its people, the lush landscapes, and the timeless traditions that spoke of deep connection to nature and spirituality. As we walked through the bustling terminal and made our way through the crowd, we couldn't shake the feeling that Bali was still with us, lingering in our minds like a beautiful dream we'd never want to wake from.

The souvenirs we carried with us—handcrafted wooden carvings, colourful textiles, aromatic coffee—were small reminders of the island's artistry and spirit. But it was the intangible things that we'd packed away most carefully: the serenity we'd found in quiet temple courtyards, the excitement of exploring hidden beaches, the joy of sharing meals and stories with fellow travellers, and the profound peace we'd felt standing on mountaintops and looking out over vast, untouched landscapes. These were the true treasures of our journey, and they'd stay with us forever.

Stepping off the plane, the energy of Kolkata felt familiar, yet somehow different, as if we had shifted inwardly during our time away. Bali had changed us in subtle ways, teaching us to slow down, to appreciate the small moments, to connect more deeply with the world around us, and most of all, to embrace the spirit of adventure with open hearts. The journey had not just been a physical one—it had been a journey of growth, reflection, and discovery.

As we made our way toward the exit, there was a quiet certainty in our hearts: Bali was not just a destination; it had become a part of us. The memories we carried with us were vivid and alive, and we knew that one day, perhaps sooner than we expected, we would return. Bali would always be there, waiting with its warmth, its beauty, and its boundless spirit, ready to welcome us back into its embrace. Until then, it would live in our hearts, an island that had enchanted us, forever changed our perspective, and left us with a deeper love for the world and the adventures yet to come.

*   *   *

Nestled in the heart of the Indonesian archipelago, Bali is much more than a tropical paradise; it's an island of mystique, beauty, and vibrant culture that captivates visitors in ways words can only attempt to convey. Bali is often called the "Island of the Gods," a nickname that hints at its sacred landscapes, harmonious culture, and spiritual ambiance. Yet, Bali's magic lies not only in its temples, beaches, and verdant rice terraces but also in the energy and traditions of its people and their deep connection to the land. It's a place where ancient spiritual practices seamlessly coexist with modern attractions, offering a truly unique travel experience that appeals to all types of travellers—from those seeking relaxation to adventure enthusiasts and culture lovers alike.

When you step foot onto Bali's shores, you are welcomed not just to a destination but into an experience where every corner of the island feels thoughtfully designed by nature and imbued with spiritual essence. Bali is a rare place that harmonizes the old and the new; you'll see it in the bustling town centres alongside tranquil temples, in the serenity of a sunrise trek on Mount Batur followed by the thrill of surfing the waves in Kuta. Each part of the island has its own distinct atmosphere, making it feel like you're traveling through a collection of unique worlds rather than one single place.

This alluring island's appeal lies in the diversity of experiences it offers, each one crafted with the backdrop of stunning natural scenery. Whether you're drawn to Bali's vast beaches, exotic jungle landscapes, or historical and religious landmarks, there's an undeniable pull that captivates travellers from every corner of the globe. The spiritual richness and hospitality that define Balinese culture invite you to take part in a way of life that values harmony and respect for both people and nature. This can be felt in the warm greetings of locals, the vibrant ceremonial offerings seen on streets and in temples, and the traditional Balinese dances that tell stories of gods, love, and nature.

A journey through Bali allows travellers to delve into a world of adventure, relaxation, and learning. For the adventurers, Bali offers an endless array of thrilling activities. Surfing, diving, trekking, and even exploring volcanic peaks provide an adrenaline-filled experience set against an awe-inspiring backdrop. For those seeking peace, the island's rich tradition of wellness and yoga is cantered in places like Ubud, where wellness retreats and spas dot the landscape, promising relaxation, renewal, and even spiritual awakening. And for culture enthusiasts, Bali is a treasure trove of artistic and cultural richness: traditional music, dance, crafts, and cuisine await, offering deep insight into the Balinese way of life.

What truly sets Bali apart is its ability to create a sense of connection. Unlike some travel destinations that are appreciated and left behind, Bali has a way of leaving a lasting imprint on its visitors. It's a place where you don't just experience beauty, but feel a part of it. Whether you're witnessing a sunrise over the rice terraces of Tegalalang, marveling at the powerful waves along the cliffside temple of Uluwatu, or exchanging smiles with a local vendor at a vibrant market, you'll find yourself absorbed into the rhythm of Bali's life.

In this guide, we will explore all that Bali has to offer, capturing the essence of why this Indonesian gem is one of the most beloved destinations in the world. From its serene temples and lush landscapes to the richness of its cuisine and the warmth of its people, we'll dive deep into what makes Bali a destination that calls travellers back again and again. For those who have yet to visit, this journey will serve as a window into the wonders that await. And for those who have already been enchanted by Bali's magic, it's a heartfelt reminder of why this island remains so cherished in the hearts of travellers around the world.

Certainly! Here's an expanded version of "The Rich Culture and Traditions of Bali" to set a captivating, in-depth tone for this section.

Bali's rich culture and traditions create a tapestry that is as mesmerizing as its landscapes. This island stands apart from the rest of Indonesia in many ways, especially with its unique Hindu-based spirituality, customs, and artistic expressions. Balinese culture is deeply intertwined with its religious beliefs, which are primarily based on Balinese Hinduism—a distinctive form of Hinduism that merges ancient Indian Hindu influences with local animist beliefs, Buddhism, and ancestor worship. This fusion has given Bali a distinctive cultural identity that is proudly displayed through its temples, ceremonies, and day-to-day customs.

Balinese Hinduism and Spiritual Practices: Unlike the predominantly Muslim population of Indonesia, the majority of Balinese people practice a unique form of Hinduism known as Agama Hindu Dharma. This spiritual tradition is based on the idea of balance and harmony with nature, making it deeply integrated into the island's lifestyle and customs. Balinese Hinduism emphasizes a connection with the divine and respect for natural elements such as earth, fire, water, and wind, which are represented through daily rituals and offerings to appease deities and ancestral spirits.

One of the most distinctive and beautiful aspects of this belief system is the "Tri Hita Karana" philosophy, which means "three causes of well-being." This philosophy promotes harmony among humans, with the natural environment, and with the divine. This balance is expressed through regular offerings, ceremonies, and community activities, helping to cultivate a deep-rooted sense of peace and respect among the Balinese people and their surroundings.

Temples and Daily Rituals: Temples are an integral part of Balinese life, both as places of worship and as centres for community gatherings. Known as "pura," these temples are scattered across the island, often set against dramatic natural backdrops such as cliffs, forests, and beaches. Among the most revered is 'Pura Besakih', known as the Mother Temple, which sits on the slopes of Mount Agung, Bali's highest peak and most sacred mountain. Other notable temples include 'Tanah Lot', perched on a rocky islet along the coastline, and 'Uluwatu Temple', which offers breathtaking cliffside views over the Indian Ocean.

The temples themselves are architectural marvels, featuring traditional Balinese designs characterized by split gates (candi bentar), pagoda-like shrines (meru towers), and intricate stone carvings. The temples are not just architectural icons; they also serve as the setting for Bali's complex religious calendar, which is filled with colourful festivals and rituals held throughout the year.

Daily offerings, known as 'canang sari', are a vital part of Balinese Hinduism and are seen everywhere—from homes and businesses to temples and streets. These small, hand-woven trays filled with flowers, rice, and incense are a beautiful sight and symbolize gratitude, respect, and an offering to both good and mischievous spirits. Visitors to Bali will often find themselves enchanted by the sight of Balinese people placing these offerings with reverence each day, a practice that fosters mindfulness and a spiritual connection to their surroundings.

<u>Vibrant Festivals and Celebrations</u>: Bali's festival calendar is a rich array of rituals and celebrations that offer visitors the chance to witness the island's culture in its most vibrant and authentic form. One of the most significant celebrations is 'Nyepi', or the Balinese New Year, a day of silence, fasting, and meditation observed across the island. In the days leading up to Nyepi, villages come alive with elaborate parades and the Ogoh-Ogoh festival, where giant, colorful effigies representing evil spirits are carried through the streets before being burned in a symbolic act of purification. On Nyepi itself, the entire island comes to a standstill as locals and visitors alike remain indoors in silent reflection, creating a rare, peaceful experience.

Another important festival is 'Galungan', a ten-day celebration that commemorates the triumph of good over evil and honours ancestral spirits. During Galungan, streets and homes are adorned with 'penjor'—tall, decorative bamboo poles draped with offerings and leaves. This is followed by "Kuningan", marking the end of the celebration and the return of ancestors to their spiritual realm.

For visitors, these festivals offer an immersive glimpse into Balinese beliefs and provide a rare opportunity to experience the community spirit and joyous atmosphere that define Bali's approach to spirituality. Joining in these events—respectfully—allows travellers to feel the powerful sense of belonging and gratitude that pervades Balinese life.

<u>Art, Dance, and Craftsmanship</u>: Bali's artistic traditions are another vital aspect of its culture. The island is renowned for its intricate wood carvings, vibrant paintings, and delicate silverwork. Each art form often draws on

religious themes, depicting stories of gods, goddesses, and legendary heroes from Hindu epics like the Ramayana and the Mahabharata. Many villages specialize in different crafts; for instance, the town of "Ubud" is famous for its painters, while "Celuk" is known for its silversmiths and "Mas" for its wood carvers.

Balinese dance is a mesmerizing art form, with performances that blend intricate finger movements, expressive gestures, and complex facial expressions to convey stories and emotions. Traditional dances like the "Legong", "Kecak", and "Barong" are deeply rooted in spiritual and cultural narratives. The Kecak dance, for example, reenacts scenes from the Ramayana and is performed by a choir of chanting men who move in unison, creating a hypnotic rhythm. Many of these dances are performed during temple ceremonies and festivals, allowing travellers to witness Bali's cultural heritage in its purest form.

The Warmth of Balinese Hospitality: One of the most striking elements of Balinese culture is the hospitality and kindness of its people. Balinese locals take pride in welcoming visitors to their island, seeing it as a part of their cultural duty. Known as "ramah Tamah", this hospitality is extended warmly to strangers and friends alike, often in the form of heartfelt smiles, polite gestures, and open invitations to witness ceremonies or join in celebrations. In Bali, you're more than just a visitor; you're welcomed as a temporary member of the community, invited to share in the island's values of peace, respect, and harmony.

Even though Bali is a major tourist destination, the locals are committed to preserving their culture and welcoming visitors in a way that feels genuine and respectful. This hospitality leaves a lasting impression on travellers and makes Bali more than just a destination but a place of connection, where the essence of "Tri Hita Karana"—the harmony between humans, nature, and spirituality—can truly be felt.

Final Thoughts on Bali's Cultural Richness: For anyone seeking a travel experience that transcends mere sightseeing, Bali offers an opportunity to immerse oneself in a culture that feels timeless, sacred, and uplifting. From the island's beautiful temples and intricate rituals to its art, dance, and warm hospitality, Bali's rich cultural heritage invites travellers to slow down, observe, and connect on a deeper level. By respecting and participating in Bali's customs, visitors not only gain a richer travel experience but also contribute to the preservation and appreciation of a culture that has captivated people for centuries.

Bali's landscapes are a breathtaking blend of verdant rice terraces, volcanic mountains, pristine beaches, and lush tropical jungles. Each corner of this Indonesian paradise presents an array of natural wonders, from tranquil forests and dramatic cliffs to vibrant coral reefs and serene lakes. The island's diverse topography, combined with its rich biodiversity, makes Bali a sanctuary for nature lovers and adventure seekers alike.

The Enchanting Rice Terraces: One of Bali's most iconic landscapes is its rice terraces, which are not only a vital part of the island's agricultural tradition but also a visual marvel. Carved into the hillsides with precision and artistry, these terraces, particularly in "Tegalalang" and "Jatiluwih", create stunning green vistas that seem to stretch endlessly. The Jatiluwih Rice Terraces, a UNESCO World Heritage Site, span over 600 hectares and are known for their "subak" irrigation system, a traditional Balinese cooperative water management method that has been practiced since the 9th century.

Strolling through the rice terraces is both peaceful and humbling, as visitors witness the harmony between nature and local farming practices that have sustained Balinese communities for generations. Early morning or late afternoon visits provide the best lighting for photography, capturing the terraces as they glow under the golden sun, reflecting off the water and creating a mystical atmosphere that feels almost otherworldly.

Majestic Volcanoes and Sacred Mountains: Bali's volcanic landscapes are as dramatic as they are beautiful, providing visitors with opportunities for adventure, stunning views, and a profound sense of the island's raw natural power. The most famous of these volcanoes is "Mount Agung", the island's highest point and most sacred peak, which reaches an elevation of 3,031 meters. Locals believe Mount Agung to be the home of the gods, and its silhouette dominates the Balinese skyline, adding a sense of reverence and awe to the surrounding region.

For those who crave adventure, trekking up "Mount Batur" offers a challenging yet accessible hike, especially popular for sunrise climbs. The journey to the top typically begins in the early hours of the morning, and as trekkers reach the summit just before dawn, they're rewarded with a view of the sun rising over a stunning panorama of clouds, volcanic craters, and the waters of "Lake Batur". The experience of watching the first light of day illuminate the island from this vantage point is a memory that many visitors describe as life-changing, highlighting the beauty and power of Bali's natural landscape.

Beaches for Every Mood: Bali is renowned for its variety of beaches, each with its own unique character, drawing surfers, sun-seekers, and beach lovers from around the world. From the bustling sands of "Kuta" and "Seminyak", with their lively beach clubs and vibrant sunset scenes, to the tranquil shores of "Sanur" and "Nusa Dua", Bali's coastline offers something for every type of traveller.

For those seeking adventure, "Uluwatu Beach" is a prime spot for surfing, with waves that attract surfers of all levels from around the world. The cliffs at Uluwatu also provide a breathtaking view, especially at sunset, when the sky transforms into shades of pink and orange over the ocean. On the other hand, "Virgin Beach" offers a more secluded and serene experience, with its white sands and clear, turquoise waters, making it perfect for swimming, snorkeling, or simply relaxing in a peaceful setting.

And for an Instagram-worthy destination, "Diamond Beach" and "Kelingking Beach" on "Nusa Penida" are hard to beat. These stunning beaches are located along dramatic cliffs, offering views that are both humbling and exhilarating. The descent down to the shore may be challenging, but the reward of seeing these secluded gems, surrounded by towering rock formations and pristine waters, is more than worth the effort.

Waterfalls and Hidden Natural Gems: Bali's landscape is also adorned with waterfalls, each more enchanting than the last. "Tegenungan Waterfall", close to Ubud, is one of the most accessible and popular, cascading down into a cool, inviting pool surrounded by lush greenery. Meanwhile, the hidden "Banyumala Twin Waterfalls" offer a more secluded experience, where visitors can immerse themselves in the raw beauty of untouched nature.

Perhaps one of the most magical waterfall experiences is found at "Tukad Cepung Waterfall", where the water cascades through a canyon, and the sunlight filters through in beams, creating a mystical, almost dream-like atmosphere. Reaching this hidden gem requires a bit of a hike, but the sight of the falls surrounded by a natural amphitheatre of cliffs makes it a captivating journey. For those who love the sound of rushing water and the thrill of discovery, exploring Bali's waterfalls is an unforgettable way to connect with the island's hidden wonders.

Marine Life and Coral Reefs: Bali's underwater world is equally captivating, attracting divers and snorkelers with its vibrant coral reefs and diverse marine life. The waters surrounding the island are home to an impressive array of creatures, from colourful tropical fish and sea turtles to manta rays and the elusive ocean sunfish, or "mola mola".

In "Nusa Penida", the "Manta Point" dive site is famous for its manta ray population, allowing divers to swim alongside these graceful giants in their natural habitat. For those less experienced in diving, "Amed" and "Tulamben" offer excellent snorkelling opportunities. The "USAT Liberty" wreck in Tulamben, a World War II ship that has become an artificial reef, is particularly popular, with its sunken structure now teeming with coral and marine life, providing a unique underwater landscape to explore.

Lush Jungles and Biodiversity: Beyond the beaches and volcanic peaks, Bali is blessed with rich, green jungles that teem with life. "Sacred Monkey Forest Sanctuary" in Ubud is a well-known spot where visitors can walk among ancient trees and observe playful long-tailed macaques in their natural environment. This forest is not only a place to encounter Bali's wildlife but also a spiritual and historical site, with ancient temples and statues that date back centuries.

For a quieter experience with nature, "West Bali National Park" offers an extensive area of tropical forests, mangroves, and savannas, providing habitats for hundreds of species, including the endangered Bali starling.

Trekking through these lesser-visited areas reveals a side of Bali that's often overlooked, offering bird-watching, hiking, and a sense of solitude in pristine natural surroundings.

Serene Lakes and Rivers: Bali's inland landscapes are equally enchanting, with serene lakes and rivers that offer peaceful retreats and opportunities for exploration. "Lake Batur", nestled at the foot of Mount Batur, is a tranquil setting, where visitors can take a boat ride across the calm waters or explore the traditional villages that dot its shores. The lake's surroundings, dominated by volcanic landscapes and mountains, create an almost mystical atmosphere that's perfect for moments of quiet reflection.

On the western side of the island, "Lake Beratan" is home to "Ulun Danu Beratan Temple", an iconic water temple that appears to float on the lake's surface, surrounded by mist and mountains. This serene setting is one of Bali's most photographed scenes, especially during sunrise when the temple and its reflections create a breathtaking image.

Endless Adventure and Exploration: Whether it's trekking through forests, diving with manta rays, or relaxing on a hidden beach, Bali offers an endless array of natural attractions for every type of traveller. Adventure seekers can find thrill in activities such as white-water rafting along the "Ayung River", cycling through villages and rice paddies, or embarking on an ATV ride through rugged terrains. For those seeking a slower pace, Bali's natural beauty offers plenty of spaces for meditation, yoga, and quiet contemplation in a lush, vibrant environment.

Bali's natural beauty is a feast for the senses, and it is as diverse as it is awe-inspiring. Each landscape—whether a towering volcano, a hidden waterfall, or a sunlit rice terrace—tells a story of harmony between the land and its people. To travel through Bali is to experience nature at its most majestic, offering visitors the chance to find peace, adventure, and wonder in a place that feels like paradise. From sunrise over Mount Batur to sunset on Kuta Beach, Bali's landscapes leave an indelible mark on the hearts of those fortunate enough to experience its extraordinary beauty.

Bali is a paradise for thrill-seekers and outdoor enthusiasts, offering a vast array of adrenaline-pumping activities that take full advantage of the island's rich natural landscape. From challenging mountain treks to water sports in pristine oceans, Bali has something to ignite the adventurous spirit of every traveller. Whether you're scaling volcanoes at sunrise, diving into the ocean to explore vibrant coral reefs, or riding through dense jungles on an ATV, Bali promises an unforgettable journey for those seeking action and adventure.

Volcano Treks and Mountaineering: For those captivated by mountain landscapes, Bali's volcanic peaks offer unparalleled trekking experiences. The two most famous mountains for trekking are "Mount Batur" and "Mount Agung". A sunrise trek to the summit of Mount Batur is one of the most popular adventures on the island, allowing trekkers to witness a breathtaking sunrise over the caldera with views that stretch across the island to the ocean. The journey usually starts in the early morning hours, with climbers navigating rocky trails under a starlit sky. When dawn breaks, the summit reveals panoramic vistas of Lake Batur and neighbouring mountains, with the warm glow of the sun gradually illuminating the landscape.

For more seasoned hikers, "Mount Agung" offers a more challenging and spiritually significant climb. As Bali's tallest peak, it rises 3,031 meters above sea level and is revered by locals, who consider it the home of the gods. The trek up Mount Agung requires physical endurance and is often undertaken with guides who understand the route and the mountain's spiritual significance. The sunrise at Mount Agung's summit is an experience of profound beauty and serenity, with views that extend across Bali and out to the neighbouring islands.

World-Class Surfing: Bali is known globally for its world-class surf spots, attracting surfers from every corner of the globe. With surf breaks suitable for every level, from beginner to advanced, Bali offers some of the best waves in Asia. "Uluwatu" is one of the most iconic surf spots on the island, boasting powerful waves and dramatic cliffs that frame the ocean. For experienced surfers, the Uluwatu breaks provide thrilling rides and challenging waves, particularly during the dry season when the swells are at their peak.

For those new to the sport, "Kuta Beach" is a perfect introduction to surfing, with long stretches of sandy shores and gentle waves ideal for beginners. Numerous surf schools in Kuta provide lessons, making it easy for newcomers to pick up the basics and catch their first waves. Other popular surfing destinations include "Padang Padang", "Canggu", and "Nusa Lembongan", each offering unique wave conditions and beautiful settings that make surfing in Bali an unforgettable adventure.

Diving and Snorkelling in Crystal Clear Waters: Bali's underwater world is just as mesmerizing as its landscapes above sea level. With diverse marine ecosystems, coral reefs, and an abundance of sea life, Bali is a dream come true for diving and snorkelling enthusiasts. "Tulamben", on Bali's northeastern coast, is famous for the "USAT Liberty wreck", a sunken World War II ship that has transformed into an artificial reef. The wreck is teeming with colourful coral and marine life, including schools of tropical fish, sea turtles, and even the elusive Mola Mola (ocean sunfish) during the right season. Diving here offers a fascinating blend of history and marine exploration.

For those who prefer to snorkel, "Amed" and "Nusa Penida" are excellent destinations. "Manta Point" in Nusa Penida is particularly popular for manta ray encounters, allowing snorkelers and divers to swim alongside these gentle giants. The crystal-clear waters of "Crystal Bay" on Nusa Penida are also ideal for snorkeling, where vibrant coral reefs and schools of fish can be easily observed close to the shore.

White-Water Rafting on Bali's Rivers: Bali's rivers offer thrilling white-water rafting experiences that allow adventurers to navigate the island's lush interiors while riding through rapids. The "Ayung River", near Ubud, is the most popular rafting destination, with gentle to moderate rapids that provide excitement without being overly intense. As rafters make their way down the river, they're surrounded by beautiful rainforest scenery, cascading waterfalls, and intricate carvings etched into the riverbanks by local artists. This journey through the Ayung River offers not only adrenaline but also a chance to experience the heart of Bali's natural beauty.

For more intense rapids, the "Telaga Waja River" in eastern Bali offers a more challenging experience. With its stronger currents and steeper drops, this river provides an exhilarating ride, especially during the rainy season when water levels are higher. White-water rafting on the Telaga Waja is perfect for those seeking a high-energy adventure that showcases Bali's dramatic landscapes.

Jungle Trekking and Hidden Waterfalls: Bali's dense jungles and hidden waterfalls make it a paradise for trekkers. Jungle trekking allows visitors to experience the island's lush vegetation, towering trees, and exotic wildlife up close. The trails around "Ubud" and "Munduk" are particularly popular for trekking, with paths that lead through rainforests, bamboo groves, and terraced rice fields. The chance to spot native flora and fauna, including vibrant butterflies, monkeys, and rare birds, adds to the experience.

Waterfall treks are also a major highlight, with Bali boasting some of the most beautiful cascades in Southeast Asia. "Tegenungan Waterfall" is close to Ubud and relatively easy to reach, while "Sekumpul Waterfall" in northern Bali is a more challenging trek but rewards hikers with stunning views and the chance to swim in pristine, cool waters. Hidden gems like "Banyumala Twin Waterfalls" and "Nungnung Waterfall" provide secluded spots where visitors can immerse themselves in nature and enjoy a refreshing dip in crystal-clear pools.

ATV Rides and Off-Road Adventures: For those who love an off-road thrill, ATV rides through Bali's rugged landscapes are an adventure that offers excitement and spectacular views. Various operators provide ATV tours that take participants through rice paddies, river crossings, muddy trails, and traditional Balinese villages, providing a close-up look at rural life on the island. Riding through the mud and navigating rocky terrain, adventurers get to experience Bali's landscape from a unique and exhilarating perspective. Many tours around "Ubud" and "Tegalalang" allow riders to explore jungles and rice terraces that are otherwise inaccessible, providing an authentic and adrenaline-pumping journey.

Paragliding and Ziplining with Panoramic Views: Paragliding over Bali's scenic coastline is an unforgettable way to experience the island's beauty from the sky. "Nusa Dua" is a popular launch point for paragliding, offering stunning views of the ocean, cliffs, and beaches below. Floating through the air, with the turquoise sea stretching to the horizon, gives adventurers a breathtaking perspective on Bali's coastal beauty. Paragliding can be done solo for experienced gliders or tandem with an instructor for those new to the sport.

For a high-flying adventure through Bali's forests, ziplining is another exhilarating activity. Various zipline parks, such as "Bali Treetop Adventure Park" in "Bedugul", offer courses through lush jungles with a series of ziplines, suspended bridges, and platforms that allow adventurers to soar through the trees like Tarzan. Ziplining is both a thrilling and family-friendly way to enjoy Bali's natural beauty while safely navigating the jungle canopy.

Cycling Tours Through Scenic Landscapes: Cycling is a popular way to explore Bali's picturesque countryside, especially around Ubud, where gentle terrain, quiet roads, and beautiful scenery make for a perfect day's ride. Many cycling tours begin near Mount Batur and take riders downhill through rice fields, villages, and small farms. Cyclists get to see a side of Bali that's often missed by those traveling by car, with opportunities to interact with locals, learn about traditional farming practices, and witness the island's slower pace of life.

The cooler climate of "Munduk" and "Bedugul" in northern Bali offers another scenic cycling destination. Here, riders can enjoy views of mountain lakes, terraced plantations, and coffee farms, with stops at local markets and temples along the way. Bali's cycling tours are designed to be accessible to most fitness levels, providing a leisurely yet engaging way to experience the island's natural and cultural wonders.

Canyoning and Cliff Jumping: For those seeking a more intense experience with nature, canyoning and cliff jumping offer a combination of adventure and natural beauty. Bali's canyons, especially those in the "Aling-Aling" area, are popular spots for these activities, allowing participants to rappel down waterfalls, jump into clear pools, and slide down natural rock formations. Canyoning tours often include guided descents through lush gorges, with the chance to discover hidden waterfalls and pools along the way. Cliff jumping is particularly thrilling, with heights ranging from a few meters to more daring drops, and always taking place under the watchful eye of experienced guides.

Horseback Riding on the Beach: Bali's beautiful beaches provide the perfect backdrop for a horseback ride, and the island offers several opportunities to ride along the coastline or through the countryside. In "Canggu" and "Seminyak", horseback riding operators allow visitors to experience the thrill of riding along sandy shores at sunset, with waves crashing nearby and the sky painted in hues of pink and orange. For a more secluded experience, riders can explore the black sand beaches of "Saba

Bay" or head inland to ride through villages, temples, and rice fields. Horseback riding in Bali is both a relaxing and memorable way to experience the island's natural landscapes.

Bali's landscape is tailor-made for adventure, offering a wide range of activities that cater to all levels of thrill-seeking. Whether it's scaling a volcano at dawn, diving among coral reefs, rafting through jungle rivers, or exploring hidden waterfalls, Bali's outdoor adventures reveal the island's incredible natural diversity. Each activity offers not just an adrenaline rush but also a way to connect with Bali's rich environment, culture, and spirit, making every adventure an unforgettable chapter in the Bali experience. For travellers with a love for the outdoors and a thirst for excitement, Bali is a paradise that promises memories and moments that will last a lifetime.

Bali is a culinary paradise that seamlessly combines Indonesian tradition, fresh local ingredients, and creative fusion to present visitors with an unforgettable gastronomic experience. With a rich tapestry of spices, flavours, and cooking techniques, Balinese cuisine offers food lovers an opportunity to taste authentic and innovative dishes alike. Bali's food culture reflects not only the island's natural abundance but also the deeply rooted traditions and customs that make each dish a unique journey in itself.

The Essence of Balinese Cuisine: At the heart of Balinese cuisine is a deep connection to the land and a strong focus on fresh ingredients, most of which are sourced locally from Bali’s fertile soils and coastal waters. Balinese cooking uses a wide variety of aromatic spices, such as turmeric, ginger, galangal, lemongrass, and chili, creating complex flavours that are earthy, spicy, and savoury. These ingredients are often combined with coconut, peanuts, and rice—an essential staple and cultural symbol on the island.

In Bali, food preparation is deeply ritualistic, with many dishes tied to spiritual and community-based customs. Traditional meals are often prepared for festivals, ceremonies, and gatherings, with particular dishes representing specific cultural values. For travellers, experiencing Balinese food is not just about tasting new flavours; it’s an immersion into the island’s spiritual practices and community life.

Iconic Balinese Dishes:

1. Babi Guling (Suckling Pig): One of Bali's most celebrated dishes, babi guling, is a ceremonial roast that exemplifies the island's mastery of spices. The pig is stuffed with a blend of spices, including turmeric, coriander, lemongrass, and garlic, then slowly roasted until the skin is crispy and the meat is tender. Traditionally served at ceremonies and feasts, babi guling can be found in local warungs (small restaurants), where it's usually served with rice, vegetables, and sambal (spicy sauce). For those interested in sampling Bali's flavors at their most authentic, babi guling is a must-try.

2. Bebek Betutu (Slow-Roasted Duck): Another specialty, bebek betutu, is a slow-cooked duck dish infused with a rich mix of spices and wrapped in banana leaves before being roasted. This dish is tender, aromatic, and full of flavour, as the slow-cooking process allows the spices to deeply penetrate the meat. Bebek betutu is usually reserved for special occasions, but several restaurants in Bali offer it for travellers seeking an authentic taste of local tradition.

3. Lawar: A staple at ceremonial meals, lawar is a mixed dish of vegetables, grated coconut, minced meat (often pork), and spices. It's seasoned with rich herbs and often includes a splash of animal blood for added flavour, though vegetarian variations are available as well. This traditional dish, with its distinctive mix of textures and spices, showcases Bali's love for bold flavors.

4. Satay Lilit: This Balinese take on satay features skewers of minced meat, typically made from fish, chicken, or pork, mixed with grated coconut, lime leaves, and a blend of spices. Satay lilit is grilled on bamboo or lemongrass sticks, which impart an additional aromatic flavour. It's served with a side of spicy sambal and often paired with rice, making it a popular and versatile dish for locals and visitors alike.

5. Nasi Campur: Nasi campur, or "mixed rice," is a comforting dish that offers a variety of flavours and textures on one plate. It includes a portion of white rice surrounded by small servings of various side dishes, such as vegetables, meats, and sambals. The diversity of ingredients in nasi campur makes it a perfect way for travellers to sample a bit of everything, from grilled meats to stir-fried vegetables, in a single meal.

6. **Nasi Goreng**: Literally meaning "fried rice," Nasi Goreng is a beloved staple made by stir-frying rice with a mix of sweet soy sauce (*kecap manis*), garlic, shallots, chili, and often a protein like chicken, shrimp, or egg. It's typically served with a fried egg on top, crispy crackers (*krupuk*), and a side of pickled vegetables, offering a perfect blend of savoury, sweet, and spicy flavours.

7. **Mee Goreng**: Meaning "fried noodles," Mee Goreng is the noodle counterpart to Nasi Goreng. Made with yellow noodles stir-fried in a similar sweet and spicy sauce, it's tossed with vegetables, eggs, and a choice of protein such as tofu, shrimp, or chicken.

Topped with fried shallots and served with lime wedges, it delivers a comforting and flavourful experience.

Fresh Seafood from Bali's Coastal Waters: Bali's proximity to the ocean means that seafood is a central part of the local cuisine. Jimbaran Bay, in particular, is famous for its beachside seafood restaurants, where diners can enjoy freshly caught fish, prawns, squid, and clams grilled to perfection. The seafood is typically seasoned with a marinade of garlic, lime, and traditional Balinese spices, then served with a side of sambal matah, a raw chili salsa that adds a burst of freshness and heat. Dining by the beach, with waves lapping nearby and a spread of fresh seafood on the table, is an essential Bali experience.

Seafood specialties such as grilled red snapper, chili crab, and prawn skewers are commonly enjoyed at open-air restaurants along the coast. For an immersive dining experience, visitors can select their preferred seafood directly from the day's catch, which is then prepared and served right on the beach. This intimate connection to fresh ingredients and local flavor is what makes Bali's seafood offerings so unique and memorable.

The Sweet Side of Bali: Balinese desserts reflect the island's tropical abundance, featuring ingredients such as coconut, palm sugar, and rice. Dadar Gulung, a rolled pancake filled with sweet coconut and palm sugar, is a popular street food treat that offers a delightful balance of chewy texture and rich sweetness. Another favourite is Bubur Injin, a black rice pudding made from glutinous black rice, coconut milk, and palm sugar, creating a creamy, mildly sweet dessert that's both comforting and flavourful.

Klepon is another unique dessert worth trying. These sticky rice balls are filled with liquid palm sugar and coated in grated coconut. When bitten into, the palm sugar filling bursts in a delightful combination of textures and flavours. Balinese desserts highlight the natural sweetness of local ingredients and provide a refreshing end to the island's flavourful meals.

Unique Dining Experiences in Bali

1. Warungs (Local Eateries): Warungs are small, family-owned eateries that offer a taste of authentic Balinese food at affordable prices. Dining in a warung is an opportunity to experience local food in a casual setting, with many warungs featuring menus that change daily based on what ingredients are available. Here, travellers can savor classic dishes like nasi goreng (fried rice), mie goreng (fried noodles), and ayam bakar (grilled chicken) while enjoying a meal that reflects the warmth and hospitality of Balinese culture.

2. Fine Dining and Fusion Cuisine: Bali's food scene is not limited to traditional dishes; the island is also known for its thriving fine dining and fusion cuisine scene. Chefs from around the world have brought their culinary expertise to Bali, creating innovative dishes that blend Indonesian flavors with international influences. High-end restaurants in Seminyak, Ubud, and Canggu offer creative takes on Balinese cuisine, incorporating modern techniques and

global ingredients to present dishes that are as visually stunning as they are delicious.

3. Farm-to-Table Experiences: Bali's fertile volcanic soil allows for an abundance of fresh produce, which has given rise to a farm-to-table movement on the island. Many restaurants in Ubud and surrounding areas source their ingredients locally, offering dishes that highlight the flavors of fresh vegetables, fruits, and herbs. Some farm-to-table venues even offer tours of their organic farms, where visitors can learn about sustainable farming practices and see firsthand how ingredients are grown.

4. Vegan and Vegetarian-Friendly Options: Bali has a flourishing vegan and vegetarian food scene, with Ubud in particular known for its health-conscious cafes and plant-based menus. Many restaurants use locally sourced vegetables, tempeh, tofu, and coconut-based products to create dishes that are both nutritious and flavorful. For those following a plant-based diet, Bali offers a wide variety of options, from smoothie bowls and salad wraps to hearty curries and tempeh burgers.

Unique Beverages to Try in Bali

1. Kopi Luwak (Civet Coffee): Known as one of the world's most exotic coffees, kopi luwak is produced using beans that have been eaten and partially digested by civet cats. The beans are then cleaned, roasted, and brewed to create a unique and smooth coffee with a distinctive taste. While kopi luwak has a controversial aspect due to animal welfare concerns, reputable farms provide

ethically sourced options for those interested in tasting this unusual coffee.

2. Bali's Herbal Elixirs: Traditional Balinese drinks such as Jamu have gained popularity for their health benefits. Jamu is an herbal tonic made from turmeric, ginger, tamarind, and honey, known for its anti-inflammatory and antioxidant properties. Many cafes and juice bars in Bali offer Jamu as part of their menu, often serving it chilled with a squeeze of lime for a refreshing and healthful beverage.
3. Bali Arak: Bali's traditional spirit, arak, is made from distilled rice or palm sap and has a strong, unique flavour. Arak can be enjoyed in cocktails or taken as a shot, though it's important to ensure that any arak consumed is from a reputable source, as some homemade arak can be unsafe. Bars and restaurants in Bali often serve arak-based cocktails with tropical ingredients like coconut water, lime, and pineapple, creating a refreshing drink that showcases the local spirit.

The Experience of Food as Culture in Bali: Beyond the flavours and ingredients, food in Bali is deeply intertwined with culture, community, and spirituality. Traditional dishes and cooking methods are passed down through generations, and meals are often prepared and shared as part of religious ceremonies or family gatherings. Eating in Bali is not just about satisfying hunger; it's a way to connect with the island's people and their values.

Many cooking classes are available for visitors interested in learning about Balinese cuisine, offering hands-on experience in preparing dishes using traditional techniques. These classes often begin with a visit to a local market, where participants can learn about Balinese ingredients and shop for fresh produce. Preparing and sharing a meal in this way is a unique way to engage with the island's culinary heritage.

In Bali, food is an essential part of life that reflects the island's natural beauty, cultural richness, and spirit of togetherness. Each meal is an opportunity to savor not only the flavours of Bali but also the warmth and vibrancy of its people. For those who enjoy exploring new cuisines and cultural connections, Bali offers a culinary experience that is as memorable as the island itself.

One of the most enchanting aspects of Bali is its people, who are renowned for their warmth, friendliness, and genuine hospitality. The Balinese culture emphasizes community, kindness, and spirituality, which are reflected in the way locals interact with visitors. This welcoming spirit transforms a trip to Bali from a simple vacation into a meaningful cultural exchange, where travellers feel not just welcomed but embraced by a deep sense of community. The openness and helpful nature of the Balinese people enrich the experience of exploring this beautiful island and leave visitors with memories of heartfelt interactions that linger long after their journey ends.

The Spirit of Hospitality: "Ramé": The Balinese people follow a cultural philosophy called "ramé," which means a lively and harmonious way of being. Ramé represents an acceptance and embrace of the joy, excitement, and busyness of life, especially within community settings. This belief in connectedness encourages people to find balance and harmony in their relationships with others. Balinese hospitality flows naturally from this philosophy, as locals go out of their way to make visitors feel comfortable, included, and at ease. This genuine care for others goes beyond formal gestures, as locals are quick to greet strangers with smiles, engage in friendly conversations, and offer assistance whenever needed.

For example, if a visitor asks for directions or needs help finding a location, locals won't just point in the general direction. Instead, they may personally accompany them or draw a simple map, often engaging in a warm chat about the best routes or nearby sights. It's not uncommon for visitors to be invited to family events, ceremonies, or meals, where they can witness firsthand the importance of sharing and togetherness in Balinese culture.

Community and Family-Centric Culture: In Bali, family and community ties are held in the highest regard. The island's social fabric is built around banjars—local community groups that play an essential role in organizing communal events, ceremonies, and gatherings. Almost every village has its own banjar, which operates as a small council where community matters are discussed, and decisions are made for the well-being of the village. Visitors who stay in smaller villages are likely to see these banjars in action, perhaps even being invited to a celebration or event hosted by a local family or the village.

Balinese families are large and interconnected, often with multiple generations living together in the same household or compound. This multi-generational structure fosters close family bonds, respect for elders, and a strong sense of responsibility toward one another. For visitors, this translates into a warm environment where they are welcomed like extended family, treated to the island's cultural wisdom, and sometimes given insights into the ancient practices that are still celebrated today.

Warm Encounters with Locals: The Market Experience: One of the most immersive ways to connect with Balinese people is through the island's vibrant markets, where locals sell fresh produce, traditional handicrafts, and street food with genuine friendliness and joy. These markets are hubs of social activity and give travellers an opportunity to interact directly with local vendors, artisans, and farmers. Bargaining is welcomed in many markets, and rather than being a transactional experience, it becomes a friendly exchange where laughter, smiles, and playful banter are often involved.

Balinese vendors are usually more than willing to share stories about their crafts, products, or family traditions with visitors, even with language barriers. They'll take the time to explain how a particular item is made, what materials are used, or how the traditional dishes they sell are prepared. This willingness to engage in conversation and share their cultural heritage with outsiders adds a personal touch to the market experience and makes visitors feel valued.

Balinese Festivals and the Spirit of Inclusivity: Bali is known for its elaborate ceremonies and festivals, where both locals and visitors can witness the vibrancy of Balinese culture. Rather than being exclusive family events, these festivals are community-wide celebrations that offer outsiders a chance to participate and learn about Balinese customs. For instance, Galungan and Kuningan are important Hindu festivals where families gather to honor their ancestors, decorate temples, and make offerings. During these celebrations, locals are often happy to explain the significance of rituals, share stories about their beliefs, and invite visitors to take part in some aspects of the festival.

One particularly welcoming aspect of these festivals is the opportunity to wear traditional Balinese clothing, such as the sarong and sash. Locals are usually eager to help visitors dress in these garments and explain the significance behind them. Many travellers find this experience enriching, as they feel like they're part of the cultural fabric of Bali, even if only for a day. By inviting visitors to participate in these ceremonies, Balinese people demonstrate an openness and hospitality that is rare to find, making travellers feel like they're part of something deeply meaningful.

Conversations with Balinese Artisans and Healers: Balinese people are known for their rich artistic traditions, and many artisans take great pride in their crafts, whether it be wood carving, painting, weaving, or silverwork. Visitors often find themselves conversing with these artists, who are more than willing to share the history and symbolism behind their work. These exchanges provide a unique insight into the island's creative traditions and the spiritual meaning that each piece holds for the artisans.

For those seeking wellness experiences, Bali also offers traditional healers known as balian, who use ancient healing techniques based on herbs, massage, and energy work. Many travellers visit these healers for traditional treatments, not only to experience Balinese healing methods but also to connect with the island's ancient practices. The balian approach their craft with humility, care, and a profound sense of respect, making visitors feel comforted and supported. Conversations with a balian reveal a deep-seated knowledge of spirituality and balance that underscores the gentle, harmonious nature of the Balinese people.

Local Guides – Custodians of Culture and Nature: Exploring Bali with a local guide is one of the best ways to experience the island authentically. Balinese guides are not just experts in geography but also custodians of local history, myths, and legends. Whether leading visitors through the lush rice terraces of Ubud or hiking up the volcanic trails of Mount Batur, local guides enrich each experience with stories of ancient temples, the importance of certain landmarks, and tales passed down through generations.

Guides often go beyond their professional duties, offering personal stories, sharing local folklore, and teaching visitors a few phrases in Balinese. They are patient, friendly, and genuinely enthusiastic about showcasing the beauty of their island. This sense of pride and dedication makes excursions around Bali feel like a journey with a friend who is deeply connected to the land and passionate about sharing its wonders with others.

A Unique Approach to Kindness – Smiles and Gestures of Respect: In Bali, gestures of respect, such as the traditional greeting "Om Swastiastu" and a slight bow with palms together, are widely practiced and add to the feeling of mutual respect between locals and visitors. Balinese people are known for their radiant smiles, which are not only expressions of friendliness but also represent their belief in maintaining peace and harmony. Visitors frequently note how the warmth of these simple gestures creates an inviting atmosphere, making even the briefest encounters memorable and heartfelt.

Smiling and kindness are inherent in Balinese culture, where people believe that showing warmth and care towards others brings good karma and reflects well on their spiritual well-being. This unique approach to hospitality ensures that even a short visit to a shop, a restaurant, or a local attraction can turn into a delightful exchange filled with warmth and friendliness. Many visitors leave Bali with a deep appreciation for the kindness they've experienced, and it's common for travellers to describe Bali not only as a beautiful place but as an island with a beautiful soul.

Leaving an Impactful Connection: For many travellers, the warm and friendly people of Bali leave a lasting impact, making them feel not only like guests but like friends and family. Locals are deeply proud of their heritage and grateful for the opportunity to share it with visitors, which is why many travellers feel a sense of belonging and connection that's rare to find elsewhere. The relationships built with locals during a trip to Bali are often some of the most cherished memories that travellers take home with them, as they're not only reminded of Bali's beauty but also the kindness of its people.

Whether it's a simple smile exchanged with a shopkeeper, a laugh shared with a guide, or a story told by an artisan, the interactions with Balinese people make every experience richer and more meaningful. By opening their lives and hearts to visitors, the people of Bali ensure that those who journey to their island leave with memories of a place that's not only stunningly beautiful but filled with genuine warmth, compassion, and a spirit of shared humanity.

Bali has long been a haven for wellness seekers from around the globe, thanks to its serene landscapes, rich spiritual heritage, and abundance of yoga and wellness centres. Often called the "Island of the Gods," Bali offers a nurturing environment where individuals can disconnect from the fast-paced demands of modern life, reconnect with themselves, and achieve a sense of inner peace. The island's wellness culture is woven into its daily life, with everything from yoga retreats and meditation workshops to holistic health practices and detox therapies offered in abundance.

Whether travellers are seasoned yogis, spiritual explorers, or simply individuals looking for a relaxing getaway, Bali's wellness retreats are renowned for providing transformative experiences in breathtaking settings. Nestled among lush jungles, terraced rice fields, and beaches with awe-inspiring ocean views, these retreats blend ancient Balinese wisdom with contemporary practices, allowing visitors to rejuvenate, restore, and find balance.

Ubud: The Spiritual Heart of Bali: Ubud is the epicentre of Bali's wellness scene, drawing travellers seeking tranquillity, healing, and self-discovery. Surrounded by dense jungles, rolling rice terraces, and sacred temples, Ubud offers an unparalleled setting for those looking to dive deeply into yoga and wellness practices. The town's spiritual energy is palpable, enhanced by the ancient traditions practiced by its residents, who frequently make offerings at their family shrines and temples to honour their Hindu gods.

Yoga studios in Ubud are plentiful, each offering unique classes and specialized programs. Some places, like the renowned Yoga Barn and Radiantly Alive, are well-known for their commitment to creating community spaces for travellers and locals alike. These studios offer a wide variety of classes, from classic Hatha and Vinyasa flows to Yin and Restorative yoga. Workshops in breathwork, sound healing, and chakra balancing are also popular here, allowing visitors to delve deeper into holistic practices that harmonize the body, mind, and spirit.

A Range of Healing Modalities – From Traditional Balinese Healing to Modern Therapies: Bali's wellness offerings are not limited to yoga alone. Many wellness centres incorporate traditional Balinese healing practices and Ayurvedic therapies, which have been practiced on the island for centuries. Balinese healers, known as "balian," use their knowledge of natural remedies, herbal medicine, and energy work to help people achieve physical, emotional, and spiritual well-being. These healers, often trained through family traditions passed down through generations, conduct sessions that include everything from herbal remedies to energy-cleansing rituals aimed at removing blockages and restoring balance to the body's energy flow.

In addition to traditional healing, Bali offers a variety of modern wellness treatments. Visitors can find everything from Ayurvedic massage and detox programs to acupuncture, reflexology, and crystal therapy. Many retreats combine these modalities, creating holistic programs that cater to the diverse needs of wellness travellers. Detox programs and juice cleanses are also popular, helping individuals remove toxins and restore vitality.

For those seeking mental clarity, mindfulness and meditation retreats are available, providing structured programs designed to calm the mind and reduce stress.

Eco-Conscious Wellness Spaces and Retreats: In recent years, Bali's wellness retreats have increasingly embraced eco-conscious practices, prioritizing sustainability and harmony with nature. Many of the island's wellness centers operate as eco-retreats, using sustainable architecture, renewable energy, and organic materials that reflect Bali's natural beauty. Accommodations are often built from bamboo or reclaimed wood, blending seamlessly with the surroundings, and feature open-air yoga shalas overlooking rice paddies, rainforests, or ocean vistas.

These retreats aim to offer a "return to simplicity" experience, where guests can fully immerse themselves in the tranquillity of nature while participating in programs that include plant-based meals, permaculture workshops, and nature-based meditations. These eco-friendly retreats often use locally sourced, organic produce for their meals, which are crafted to nourish both the body and soul. The emphasis on sustainability and holistic living makes Bali's wellness retreats feel uniquely integrated into the environment, where guests not only benefit personally but contribute to the preservation of the island's beauty and culture.

Sound Healing, Breathwork, and Meditation Practices: Apart from yoga, Bali has become known for its powerful sound healing and breathwork sessions. Many wellness centres in Ubud and other parts of the island hold weekly sound healing ceremonies, where participants can relax to the vibrations of gongs, singing bowls, chimes, and drums. Sound healing is believed to work at a vibrational level, helping to release stress, anxiety, and tension in the body. Visitors often report feeling deeply relaxed and emotionally cleansed after these sessions, and some find it a powerful form of meditation.

Breathwork, another popular offering in Bali, involves guided breathing exercises aimed at helping individuals release deep-seated emotions, increase oxygen flow, and boost energy levels. The breath is considered a powerful tool for connecting the mind and body, and many practitioners view breathwork as a transformative experience. Combined with meditation, these practices foster mindfulness and self-awareness, helping individuals overcome inner obstacles and gain clarity.

Private Villas and Personalized Wellness Programs: For those looking for a more intimate and personalized experience, Bali offers a wealth of private wellness villas and boutique retreats that cater to individual needs. These private retreats provide custom-designed programs, often starting with an initial consultation to determine guests' personal wellness goals, whether it be stress relief, improved physical fitness, or spiritual growth. Private yoga and meditation sessions, tailored meal plans, and one-on-one healing treatments with trained therapists make these programs highly personalized, allowing visitors to work at their own pace in a tranquil setting.

Many of these private wellness villas are designed to offer complete seclusion, providing guests with a sanctuary where they can enjoy solitude while having access to professional wellness support. Whether nestled in Ubud's lush jungles, perched on a cliff overlooking the ocean in Uluwatu, or set within the quiet village life of Sidemen, these villas offer unparalleled privacy and luxury. Guests can relax in private pools, meditate on sun-dappled terraces, and receive massages on-site while enjoying sweeping views of the natural beauty that surrounds them.

Transformative Wellness Retreats and Yoga Teacher Training: For many visitors, wellness retreats in Bali go beyond mere relaxation; they are an opportunity for personal transformation. Many centres offer long-term retreats, some lasting several weeks or even months, where guests can undergo significant lifestyle changes. These transformative retreats often combine daily yoga and meditation with other holistic practices, such as nutritional counselling, personal coaching, and journaling. Many participants report profound changes in their mental, physical, and spiritual well-being, feeling more connected to themselves and inspired to live more intentionally.

Bali is also a popular destination for yoga teacher training (YTT) programs, attracting people from all over the world who wish to deepen their practice and potentially teach yoga professionally. These programs, often accredited by the Yoga Alliance, provide comprehensive instruction in yoga philosophy, anatomy, and teaching techniques. Training programs in Bali usually include a strong emphasis on personal growth, community building, and spiritual practice, making them ideal for those seeking a transformative experience. The natural beauty and spiritual energy of the island enhance the training experience, offering participants an inspiring environment for self-reflection and growth.

Embracing the Balinese Philosophy of "Tri Hita Karana": Bali's wellness culture is deeply influenced by the Balinese philosophy of Tri Hita Karana, which means "three causes of well-being." This philosophy emphasizes three main aspects: harmony with God, harmony with others, and harmony with nature. The people of Bali integrate this philosophy into their daily lives, striving for balance and respect in all aspects of their existence. Wellness retreats in Bali often incorporate the principles of Tri Hita Karana, helping visitors connect to this ancient philosophy through daily rituals, gratitude practices, and mindful living.

Visitors are encouraged to participate in offerings and prayer rituals, which help cultivate gratitude and humility. This emphasis on connection, not only with oneself but with others and the natural world, resonates with many visitors, giving them a sense of grounding and fulfilment. Tri Hita Karana teaches that true wellness can only be achieved through balance, making it a powerful framework for the wellness experiences offered across the island.

A Journey of Healing and Self-Discovery: For many visitors, the experience of a wellness retreat in Bali becomes a life-changing journey of healing and self-discovery. The tranquillity of the island's natural landscapes, combined with the compassionate teachings of Balinese healers and wellness practitioners, creates an environment that is conducive to personal transformation. Whether it's through a yoga class overlooking the rice fields, a sound bath in a jungle sanctuary, or a quiet meditation session on the beach, visitors often find themselves on a path toward greater self-awareness, emotional healing, and spiritual growth.

Bali's wellness retreats offer a unique opportunity to step away from the demands of everyday life, reconnect with nature, and realign with personal values. The island's serene atmosphere, combined with its wealth of wellness offerings, encourages visitors to slow down, breathe deeply, and embark on a journey that nourishes the soul. In Bali, wellness is not just a trend—it is a way of life, a practice rooted in respect, spirituality, and the belief that every individual deserves peace, happiness, and harmony.

Affordable Luxury and Unique Accommodations: Embrace Bali's Hospitality

Bali is celebrated worldwide for offering luxury accommodations that are often surprisingly affordable, allowing travellers to experience upscale, boutique lodgings and unique architectural stays without breaking the bank. From opulent beachside resorts and eco-conscious retreats in the jungle to secluded cliffside villas and bamboo treehouses, Bali provides a diverse range of options that cater to all kinds of travellers, from honeymooners seeking romance to families on a dream holiday. Bali's accommodations offer not just a place to stay, but a truly immersive experience that blends style, comfort, and Balinese charm.

Whether travellers choose to stay in bustling areas like Seminyak, surrounded by lively beach clubs, or in the quiet, spiritual town of Ubud, Bali's accommodation scene stands out for its commitment to exceptional service, unique design, and affordability. Luxurious doesn't always mean high-cost in Bali; here, you can indulge in lavish amenities like private pools, on-call butlers, and panoramic views at prices that would be unimaginable in most other top travel destinations. This accessible luxury is one of the many reasons Bali has become such a popular destination for tourists from all walks of life.

Beachside Villas and Oceanfront Resorts: Imagine waking up to the sound of waves crashing on the shore, with an uninterrupted view of the ocean stretching beyond your private infinity pool. Bali's beachside accommodations, particularly in places like Nusa Dua, Seminyak, and Jimbaran, offer exactly this experience, combining the allure of tropical luxury with the laid-back charm of coastal living. Guests can find oceanfront resorts that rival any five-star destination, complete with sprawling pools, beachfront access, gourmet restaurants, and world-class spas, all while remaining surprisingly affordable compared to similar stays in other international locales.

Many oceanfront resorts in Bali also feature beachside yoga sessions, sunset cocktails, and access to private beach clubs where guests can relax in style. The staff at these resorts are known for their warmth and attention to detail, ensuring guests feel pampered and welcome from the moment they arrive. Seminyak, for instance, is known for its trendy, upscale resorts with a vibrant beach culture and easy access to chic restaurants, boutiques, and nightlife. On the other hand, Nusa Dua offers a more secluded and relaxed experience, ideal for honeymooners and those seeking peace, privacy, and exclusivity.

Jungle Retreats and Rice Terrace Escapes: For travellers who crave a more secluded experience, the lush jungles and terraced rice fields of Ubud provide a magical escape from the bustle of everyday life. Ubud is home to some of Bali's most beautiful accommodations, often nestled among tropical greenery and traditional Balinese temples. Here, jungle retreats and villas are designed to blend seamlessly with the surrounding nature, using natural materials like bamboo, teak, and rattan. Many of these villas offer stunning views of the Ayung River Valley, infinity pools overlooking verdant rice paddies, and open-air bathrooms that allow guests to shower under the stars.

One standout accommodation option in Ubud is the eco-lodge concept, which emphasizes sustainable architecture and eco-conscious practices. Eco-lodges are designed to harmonize with Bali's landscapes while minimizing their environmental impact. These lodges often utilize solar energy, recycle rainwater, and serve farm-to-table meals with ingredients sourced from nearby organic farms. Staying in an eco-lodge allows guests to immerse themselves in Bali's natural beauty while supporting sustainable tourism.

For a truly unique experience, some jungle retreats even offer treehouse accommodations, where rooms are elevated into the canopy, providing guests with an immersive nature experience. These treehouses often feature wraparound decks, hammocks, and cozy nooks where guests can relax and take in the breathtaking forest views. Staying in a treehouse in the jungles of Bali allows travellers to feel like they're part of the island's lush landscape, making for an unforgettable experience.

Cliffside Villas and Seaside Hideaways: For those seeking a more dramatic landscape, Bali's cliffsides offer some of the island's most stunning accommodations. Areas like Uluwatu and Pecatu, located along Bali's southern coast, are home to a range of cliffside villas that provide panoramic views of the Indian Ocean. Perched on the edge of towering limestone cliffs, these villas are the epitome of luxury and privacy, often featuring private infinity pools, outdoor dining areas, and expansive terraces perfect for watching the sunset over the sea.

Cliffside accommodations are ideal for travellers looking to indulge in both adventure and relaxation. Many of these villas are located near famous surf breaks, making them popular among surfing enthusiasts who want easy access to Bali's waves. At the same time, the serene setting provides a quiet escape where guests can unwind and enjoy the scenery. The hospitality teams at these cliffside retreats are dedicated to providing personalized services, from arranging candlelit dinners on the terrace to offering guided yoga sessions overlooking the ocean.

Unique Balinese Architecture – Bamboo Houses and Traditional Villas: Bali's unique sense of style extends into its architecture, with many accommodations showcasing traditional Balinese design or innovative structures made from bamboo. Some of the island's most distinctive stays are bamboo houses, located in lush jungles or on the outskirts of Ubud. Bamboo, a renewable and resilient material, is used to create multi-story structures with intricate designs, open layouts, and impressive craftsmanship. These bamboo houses offer a sense of calmness and connection to nature, with open-air living spaces that allow fresh air to flow through, along with views of the jungle or rice fields.

Traditional Balinese villas are also popular among travellers, often featuring distinctive thatched roofs, stone carvings, and lush gardens with koi ponds. These villas incorporate local craftsmanship, with many details hand-carved by Balinese artisans. The dccor inside traditional villas typically includes vibrant textiles, antique furniture, and intricate wooden carvings, making each space feel both luxurious and authentic. Many traditional villas also come with private pools, outdoor pavilions, and alfresco dining spaces, allowing guests to enjoy Bali's pleasant tropical weather.

Affordable Boutique Hotels and Guesthouses: One of Bali's most attractive qualities as a travel destination is its ability to offer luxury and style across a range of budgets. Boutique hotels and guesthouses throughout the island provide travellers with comfortable, stylish accommodations that don't sacrifice quality for affordability. These smaller, independently-owned hotels often focus on personalized service and unique decor, creating a homey, intimate environment where guests feel welcomed and valued.

In towns like Canggu, Sanur, and Amed, boutique hotels cater to a variety of interests and aesthetics. Many are surfer-friendly, offering equipment rentals and classes, while others cater to wellness travellers with onsite yoga studios and organic cafes. Boutique hotels in Bali frequently incorporate local art, handicrafts, and furnishings that reflect the island's rich culture, creating spaces that feel authentically Balinese. Staying at a boutique hotel is an excellent option for travellers who want a unique experience without the price tag of a luxury resort.

Wellness Retreats and Spa Resorts – A Sanctuary for the Soul: For travellers seeking a rejuvenating experience, Bali's wellness resorts provide a peaceful sanctuary where guests can focus on health, relaxation, and inner well-being. Many wellness resorts are set in tranquil locations, such as the serene jungles of Ubud or the quiet beaches of Canggu. These resorts often offer comprehensive wellness packages, including daily yoga classes, meditation sessions, detox programs, and access to spa facilities.

Spa treatments in Bali are world-class, with many resorts offering traditional Balinese massage, facials, and herbal therapies designed to relax and restore.

Wellness resorts prioritize holistic healing, combining luxury with opportunities for personal growth and mindfulness. Private villas with serene gardens, organic dining options, and expert wellness practitioners allow guests to rejuvenate both body and mind in beautiful, nature-centric settings. This combination of luxury and wellness, often at a fraction of the cost found elsewhere, has made Bali one of the most sought-after wellness destinations in the world.

Family-Friendly Villas and Accommodations for Large Groups: Bali is a fantastic destination for families and groups, with plenty of family-friendly villas and large accommodations designed to cater to multiple guests. These villas often include several bedrooms, spacious living areas, and private pools, providing ample space for relaxation and play. Family-friendly villas are usually located in quieter areas like Sanur or Nusa Dua, where families can enjoy safe beaches, calm waters, and access to nearby attractions.

Many family-oriented accommodations also offer services such as babysitting, kids' clubs, and special activities, allowing parents to relax and enjoy their vacation while children are entertained. For larger groups, Bali's villas offer the perfect combination of privacy and communal space, allowing families or friends to stay together in a shared setting while still having access to luxurious amenities.

Exceptional Service and Hospitality: A defining feature of Bali's accommodations is the warmth and hospitality of its people. Balinese culture is rooted in a deep respect for guests, and this is reflected in the impeccable service provided at most hotels, villas, and resorts. Guests often note how attentive, courteous, and genuinely caring the staff are, going above and beyond to ensure a memorable experience. Many accommodations offer personalized services, including custom meal preparation, local tour arrangements, and cultural experiences such as cooking classes or traditional Balinese ceremonies.

Staying in Bali offers more than just comfort; it provides a unique cultural experience that leaves a lasting impression. From the gentle hospitality to the artfully designed spaces and serene natural surroundings, Bali's accommodations are part of what makes the island so special. Each stay is thoughtfully curated to reflect the island's natural beauty, artistic heritage, and dedication to exceptional service, allowing travellers to feel deeply connected to the place and its people.

Accessible Luxury for Every Traveller: The ability to enjoy world-class accommodations at accessible prices is one of Bali's biggest draws. The island's range of lodging options—from luxury cliffside villas and intimate jungle retreats to budget-friendly boutique hotels—ensures that every traveller can find something that suits their style and budget. Bali's accommodation scene is a testament to the island's welcoming spirit, offering unique experiences, stunning architecture, and a touch of luxury at prices that make this paradise island accessible to more people.

With such a broad array of options, Bali's accommodations invite every visitor to experience the island's renowned hospitality and natural beauty in a way that suits their personal preferences and budget. Whether you're seeking an indulgent escape, a wellness retreat, or an adventure-filled holiday, Bali has a place that will make your stay unforgettable.

Bali's Role as a Digital Nomad Haven: A Thriving Hub for Remote Work and Creativity

Bali has firmly established itself as a top destination for digital nomads, thanks to its unique combination of stunning natural beauty, affordable living costs, high-quality coworking spaces, and a welcoming culture. For freelancers, entrepreneurs, and remote workers, Bali isn't just a holiday destination—it's a place where professional and personal growth flourish in a vibrant, international community. The island has created an ecosystem that caters to those who want to blend productivity with an inspiring lifestyle, making it a favourite for creative professionals, tech enthusiasts, and digital nomads from around the globe.

In recent years, areas like Ubud, Canggu, and Seminyak have become digital nomad hotspots, each offering its own unique vibe, infrastructure, and amenities to support remote work. Bali's rise as a digital nomad haven is no accident; it's the result of a welcoming policy environment, strategic investments in coworking infrastructure, and a naturally inspiring setting that encourages innovation, collaboration, and creativity. The island's friendly visa policies, combined with a high quality of life at a relatively low cost, make it a sustainable option for long-term stays.

Affordable Living and Comfortable Lifestyle: One of the most attractive aspects of Bali for digital nomads is its affordability, allowing visitors to maintain a comfortable and balanced lifestyle without breaking the bank. Accommodation in Bali ranges from budget-friendly guesthouses to luxurious villas with private pools, making it easy for remote workers to find a space that meets their needs and budget. In popular digital nomad hubs like Canggu and Ubud, it's common to find long-term rental options at affordable prices, which often include amenities like high-speed internet, laundry services, and daily housekeeping. This cost-effective lifestyle allows digital nomads to focus on their work, pursue passion projects, and enjoy the local culture.

The cost of living is also lower compared to major Western cities, enabling digital nomads to enjoy high-quality food, healthcare, and recreational activities without financial stress. With a fraction of the budget, they might need elsewhere, they can indulge in everything from daily yoga sessions to fine dining, spa treatments, and weekend getaways to nearby islands. In Bali, the pursuit of a balanced life, where work seamlessly integrates with relaxation and self-care, becomes achievable.

High-Quality Coworking Spaces and Fast Internet: Bali's coworking spaces are among the best in the world, offering high-speed internet, comfortable workstations, and a sense of community. Ubud, Canggu, and Seminyak each boast numerous coworking spaces designed specifically with digital nomads in mind. Spaces like Hubud in Ubud, Dojo Bali in Canggu, and Outpost in various locations provide not only the essentials for productivity—like quiet work zones, private meeting rooms, and reliable Wi-Fi—but also a social environment that promotes networking and collaboration. These coworking spaces often feature open-air designs and incorporate Balinese aesthetics, creating inspiring and calming environments that encourage both creativity and focus.

Reliable, fast internet access is a must for remote workers, and Bali's coworking spaces deliver just that. In addition to coworking spaces, many cafes and restaurants in nomad hotspots provide stable internet connections and are designed to accommodate working visitors, with outlets, comfortable seating, and delicious menus to keep energy levels high. With such resources readily available, digital nomads can focus on their work while enjoying the flexibility to explore the island's beautiful locations.

Networking, Community Events, and Learning Opportunities: The digital nomad scene in Bali is not just about solo work; it's also about community, networking, and continuous learning. In places like Canggu and Ubud, weekly meet-ups, workshops, and skill-sharing sessions provide digital nomads with opportunities to learn from each other, collaborate, and create meaningful connections. These events are usually hosted by coworking spaces, cafes, or wellness centres, and cover a variety of topics—from business strategy and marketing to mindfulness and wellness. This vibrant community atmosphere makes Bali a rich environment for professional development, creative collaboration, and personal growth.

Networking events in Bali often attract an international mix of people from diverse industries, allowing for cross-industry exchanges that spark innovation and inspiration. For instance, someone working in tech may meet a digital marketer, an artist, or a wellness coach, leading to new collaborations or ideas they may not have encountered elsewhere. Bali has become an incubator for creative and entrepreneurial minds who thrive on exchanging ideas, mentoring, and building new projects. These connections often extend beyond professional life, as digital nomads frequently become friends, travel companions, or collaborators on future ventures.

Emphasis on Work-Life Balance and Wellness: One of the primary reasons digital nomads flock to Bali is its emphasis on wellness and a balanced lifestyle. Work-life balance is easier to achieve in Bali, where there are countless opportunities to unwind and recharge after a productive day. With yoga studios, meditation retreats, surf schools, and nature hikes readily available, Bali allows digital nomads to seamlessly integrate wellness into their daily routines. Many coworking spaces even offer yoga classes, mindfulness workshops, and wellness programs as part of their membership packages, promoting a culture of health and well-being.

The island's natural beauty also encourages an outdoor lifestyle that is essential for mental clarity and stress relief. Digital nomads can spend their mornings working and their afternoons exploring Bali's beaches, temples, or rice terraces, creating a balanced and fulfilling routine. This blend of productivity and leisure is a rare and attractive quality that keeps digital nomads returning to Bali year after year. Bali's wellness culture aligns with the growing trend of self-care among remote workers, making it an ideal destination for those who prioritize their mental and physical health alongside their professional goals.

Supportive Visa Policies and Long-Term Stay Options: Bali's favourable visa policies have made it easier for digital nomads to stay for extended periods. The Social and Business Visas allow for stays of up to six months, and there are various visa-on-arrival options for shorter-term travellers. Recently, Indonesian authorities have also proposed a digital nomad visa that would allow remote workers to stay in Bali for even longer without facing tax implications, making it even more appealing for those who want to establish a more permanent base on the island.

These flexible visa options have allowed many digital nomads to treat Bali as a temporary home, giving them ample time to explore the island, integrate into the local community, and develop long-term projects. By offering visa options that cater specifically to remote workers, Bali has positioned itself as one of the most accessible and attractive locations for digital nomads. This welcoming attitude from the local government has contributed to Bali's rise as a global hub for remote work, attracting digital nomads who seek a stable and accommodating environment for extended stays.

Environmental Awareness and Sustainability Initiatives: Bali's role as a digital nomad hub has also fostered a growing awareness of environmental sustainability among its community. Many digital nomads are eco-conscious travellers who prioritize destinations that share their values. As a response, Bali's businesses, particularly in the hospitality and coworking industries, have adopted sustainable practices to reduce waste and minimize their environmental impact. Many coworking spaces, cafes, and accommodations have adopted eco-friendly practices such as banning single-use plastics, offering reusable water stations, and promoting local, organic products.

Digital nomads in Bali are often active participants in environmental initiatives, organizing beach clean-ups, supporting local conservation efforts, and advocating for sustainable tourism. This eco-conscious culture aligns well with Bali's commitment to preserving its natural beauty and supporting local communities. This shared dedication to sustainability has further solidified Bali's appeal as a responsible and forward-thinking destination for digital nomads.

Cultural Immersion and Appreciation for Local Customs: Living in Bali as a digital nomad offers a unique opportunity to experience Balinese culture in an authentic and immersive way. Many digital nomads take an active interest in learning about the island's customs, attending local ceremonies, and supporting local artisans. Bali's cultural richness—its temples, festivals, and traditional art forms—offers digital nomads a chance to explore beyond their work and connect with the island's heritage.

Balinese locals are known for their welcoming and friendly attitude toward foreign visitors, creating a warm environment for digital nomads to feel at home. This cross-cultural exchange enriches the digital nomad experience, as it allows for meaningful connections with Balinese people and an understanding of the island's customs and way of life. Many digital nomads participate in local activities, like cooking classes, language lessons, and volunteering, fostering a spirit of cultural respect and appreciation.

Opportunities for Professional Growth and Skill Development: Beyond the networking events and coworking spaces, Bali provides digital nomads with ample opportunities for skill development and professional growth. The island's thriving community of freelancers, entrepreneurs, and creatives has led to the emergence of specialized workshops, mentorship programs, and online courses that digital nomads can access to sharpen their skills and advance their careers. Some coworking spaces even offer formal programs, such as startup incubators and business coaching, providing a platform for digital nomads to take their professional lives to the next level.

The collaborative atmosphere among Bali's digital nomad community means that knowledge-sharing is common, whether through formal workshops or casual conversations over coffee. As a result, Bali is a place where digital nomads not only work but also evolve, expand their skillsets, and gain new perspectives that they can carry forward in their careers.

A Global Digital Nomad Hub for the Future: Bali's role as a digital nomad haven is a testament to its unique blend of affordability, infrastructure, and inspiring environment. The island offers the perfect setting for those who seek a professional life that integrates seamlessly with personal wellness, creativity, and community. Bali's future as a digital nomad hub looks bright, with continued investment in infrastructure, a supportive community, and government policies that facilitate long-term stays. With its ideal balance of work, leisure, and wellness, Bali has set a new standard for what it means to be a digital nomad, offering a quality of life that's as fulfilling as it is productive.

In recent years, Bali has evolved into a leader in sustainable and responsible tourism, aiming to protect its natural and cultural assets while accommodating millions of annual visitors. With its fragile ecosystems, diverse marine life, and vibrant traditions, Bali faces a unique challenge: how to welcome travellers while preserving the island's delicate beauty and rich heritage for future generations. Responding to this challenge, the Balinese government, local communities, and tourism industry have adopted a range of innovative strategies and practices to create a tourism model that respects the environment, empowers local people, and promotes cultural preservation.

This shift toward sustainable tourism is not only important for maintaining Bali's allure as a top travel destination, but it also reflects the growing global consciousness among travellers. Today's tourists, more aware than ever of their environmental impact, increasingly seek destinations that prioritize ethical and sustainable practices. Bali has embraced this trend wholeheartedly, offering visitors numerous ways to travel responsibly and contribute positively to the island's future.

Emphasis on Eco-Friendly Accommodations: Bali is home to numerous eco-friendly accommodations that aim to minimize environmental impact and provide travellers with a sustainable experience. From boutique hotels and resorts that incorporate green architecture to eco-lodges built from sustainable materials, Bali offers a range of lodging options for environmentally conscious travellers. Many eco-resorts have adopted energy-saving measures such as solar panels, rainwater harvesting systems, and natural ventilation to reduce their carbon footprint. Additionally, these accommodations prioritize waste reduction, often banning single-use plastics and providing reusable containers, straws, and water bottles.

The architectural design of many eco-friendly resorts in Bali integrates harmoniously with the surrounding landscape. For example, some resorts in Ubud and Seminyak are designed to blend into the rainforest or rice paddies, preserving the natural scenery and ensuring minimal disturbance to wildlife. By choosing eco-conscious accommodations, travellers in Bali can enjoy comfort and luxury while contributing to a sustainable tourism industry.

Waste Management and Plastic-Free Initiatives: Plastic waste has long been a challenge for Bali, especially as tourism has increased. However, the island has taken significant steps toward reducing plastic usage and promoting responsible waste management. Bali was one of the first regions in Indonesia to implement a ban on single-use plastics in 2019, including plastic bags, straws, and Styrofoam. This landmark regulation encouraged local businesses, hotels, and restaurants to adopt eco-friendly alternatives, such as biodegradable packaging and reusable bags.

Several local organizations are also dedicated to tackling waste issues head-on. For example, Bye Bye Plastic Bags, founded by two Balinese teenagers, has been instrumental in raising awareness about plastic pollution and encouraging locals and visitors alike to reduce their plastic use. The organization hosts beach clean-ups and campaigns, inspiring both the community and travellers to take responsibility for the island's cleanliness. Through these efforts, Bali is making strides toward a cleaner, greener future, and tourists are encouraged to participate in local clean-up activities, reinforcing the importance of waste reduction.

Marine Conservation and Eco-Friendly Water Activities: With its rich marine biodiversity, Bali has taken serious measures to protect its underwater ecosystems, which are essential not only for tourism but also for the livelihoods of many local communities. Coral reefs, marine animals, and pristine beaches are integral to Bali's tourism appeal, making marine conservation a top priority. Many dive centres and tour operators now offer eco-friendly diving and snorkelling tours that educate participants on coral preservation, responsible marine interactions, and waste disposal while on the water.

Nusa Penida, Menjangan Island, and Pemuteran are just a few locations where visitors can experience Bali's vibrant underwater life in a sustainable way. Coral restoration projects are underway in many areas, with volunteers and tourists welcome to participate in activities like planting coral fragments or cleaning up reefs. Additionally, strict guidelines are enforced to prevent damage to coral and to promote respectful behaviour around marine animals. Sustainable tourism initiatives also extend to water sports, with operators promoting eco-friendly alternatives, such as paddleboarding and kayaking, instead of motorized activities that could harm marine life.

Promoting Sustainable Dining and Local Produce: Sustainable tourism in Bali also encompasses the culinary scene, with an emphasis on locally sourced, organic ingredients that support Balinese farmers and reduce the carbon footprint associated with imported goods. Many restaurants and cafes, especially in areas like Ubud and Canggu, have embraced the "farm-to-table" philosophy, sourcing produce directly from nearby farms and organic gardens. This trend has resulted in a thriving market for local ingredients, from organic vegetables and fruits to Balinese spices, creating a mutually beneficial relationship between the tourism sector and local agriculture.

Bali's sustainable dining movement also emphasizes plant-based options, which are not only healthy but also reduce the environmental impact of meat production. Restaurants that promote vegetarian and vegan cuisine, such as Sayuri Healing Food in Ubud and Peloton Supershop in Canggu, are popular among travellers looking to support eco-friendly practices. Additionally, some establishments have adopted zero-waste principles, where leftover food is composted, and excess ingredients are repurposed creatively. For travellers, dining at these establishments is a way to enjoy Bali's unique flavors while supporting local communities and reducing their environmental footprint.

Cultural Tourism – Respecting and Preserving Balinese Traditions: Bali's commitment to sustainable tourism extends beyond environmental initiatives to the preservation of its rich cultural heritage. Local communities and cultural organizations work hard to ensure that Balinese traditions are respected and celebrated. Programs that promote cultural tourism offer visitors authentic experiences, such as traditional dance performances, cooking classes, and craft workshops, while educating them about Balinese customs and values.

In addition, some cultural tourism initiatives focus on educating visitors about the Balinese philosophy of Tri Hita Karana, which emphasizes harmony between people, nature, and spirituality. By participating in these activities, travellers gain a deeper understanding of Bali's unique way of life, fostering a sense of respect and appreciation for the culture. This approach to cultural tourism also benefits the local community by providing economic opportunities, allowing traditional artisans, dancers, and musicians to share their talents while earning a living.

Empowering Local Communities Through Tourism: One of the most significant aspects of responsible tourism in Bali is its focus on empowering local communities. Many tourism businesses, from hotels to tour companies, have adopted community-based tourism models that actively involve and benefit local residents. For instance, visitors can book village tours, where they can learn about Balinese farming practices, participate in rice planting, and enjoy traditional meals prepared by local families. This immersive experience provides travellers with insights into Balinese daily life while directly supporting the local economy.

Organizations such as Bali Ecotourism Association and Friends of National Parks Foundation collaborate with local communities to create sustainable tourism opportunities that promote environmental conservation and cultural preservation. These programs not only benefit locals financially but also create educational opportunities for children and contribute to community development projects. Responsible travellers in Bali are encouraged to support these initiatives, making a positive impact through their travels and helping to uplift the communities they visit.

Supporting Wildlife and Nature Conservation Efforts: With its diverse ecosystems, Bali is home to numerous flora and fauna that require protection from the pressures of tourism and development. Several sanctuaries, such as the Bali Bird Park and the Sacred Monkey Forest Sanctuary in Ubud, are dedicated to preserving Bali's wildlife and educating visitors on responsible interactions with animals. The Bali Wildlife Rescue Centre is another organization that works to rescue and rehabilitate endangered species, offering opportunities for visitors to learn about the importance of animal conservation.

For those passionate about wildlife protection, volunteering with conservation programs can be a rewarding way to contribute to Bali's sustainable tourism efforts. Programs focused on sea turtle conservation, for example, provide hands-on opportunities for travellers to help protect nesting sites and care for baby turtles until they are ready to return to the ocean. By participating in these programs, tourists play an active role in protecting Bali's natural heritage and supporting biodiversity on the island.

Environmental Education and Awareness Programs: Education is a fundamental component of Bali's sustainable tourism strategy. Numerous initiatives and organizations are dedicated to raising awareness about environmental issues and encouraging responsible behaviour among visitors. Many eco-friendly resorts and tour operators offer workshops on topics such as ocean conservation, waste management, and sustainable agriculture. These educational programs often include hands-on activities, such as beach clean-ups, organic gardening, and tree planting, which allow travellers to learn and actively contribute to Bali's environmental preservation efforts.

Moreover, organizations like Green School Bali have become international symbols of sustainability and eco-conscious education. The school offers a unique learning experience cantered on sustainability, attracting both students and educators from around the world. Visitors are welcome to tour the campus, which is built entirely from bamboo and other natural materials, serving as a model for sustainable architecture. Through these programs, Bali is fostering a global community of environmentally conscious individuals who can take their knowledge and values beyond the island.

The Future of Sustainable Tourism in Bali: As Bali continues to grow as a popular travel destination, its commitment to sustainable and responsible tourism is more critical than ever. The island's leaders, local communities, and tourism industry are united in their efforts to create a model of tourism that respects the environment, preserves cultural heritage, and benefits local residents. Initiatives to limit visitor numbers in ecologically sensitive areas, promote eco-friendly transportation, and educate travellers about responsible tourism are part of Bali's long-term vision for sustainable growth.

For travellers, choosing to support Bali's sustainable tourism initiatives allows them to enjoy the island's beauty while contributing positively to its future. By respecting local customs, reducing waste, supporting eco-friendly businesses, and participating in conservation efforts, visitors play a vital role in Bali's sustainability journey. This commitment to responsible tourism ensures that future generations of travellers will be able to experience Bali's magic, while local communities continue to thrive and the island's natural treasures remain protected.

In embracing sustainable tourism, Bali has set an inspiring example for other destinations worldwide, proving that it is possible to balance tourism with environmental stewardship and cultural preservation. As Bali continues its journey toward a greener, more sustainable future, it invites travellers to join in, explore responsibly, and leave a positive mark on this extraordinary island paradise.

Reflecting on a journey through Bali is more than recounting destinations and experiences; it's about understanding the profound impact the island has on the soul. For many travellers, Bali transcends the concept of a mere holiday location—it becomes a place of self-discovery, an environment that inspires inner growth, and a sanctuary where natural beauty, culture, spirituality, and humanity converge. With every moment spent amid the island's enchanting landscapes, rich traditions, and heartfelt people, travellers often find themselves not just observing Bali but truly absorbing it, leaving the island with a sense of fulfilment, gratitude, and a transformed outlook on life.

Embracing the Spirit of Adventure and Discovery: Bali encourages travellers to embrace curiosity and dive into diverse experiences that push the boundaries of comfort and familiarity. From trekking up the towering Mount Batur before dawn to witnessing the sun's first rays light up the active volcano, or navigating hidden trails leading to secret waterfalls tucked in dense jungles, Bali ignites a spirit of exploration that leaves travellers with a deep sense of accomplishment and wonder. Each adventure is a reminder of the resilience required to reach these stunning places, instilling a sense of humility and respect for nature's raw power and beauty.

Beyond physical exploration, travellers often find themselves exploring aspects of their personality and resilience they might not have recognized before. Bali's natural wonders—its towering cliffs, vast ocean, and ancient rainforests—teach travellers to confront the unknown with an open heart. Leaving one's comfort zone becomes a natural part of experiencing Bali, and through it, travellers frequently uncover newfound courage and confidence within themselves.

Immersing in Balinese Culture and Gaining a New Perspective on Life: A transformative aspect of Bali is its vibrant cultural heritage that pervades every facet of life. Travellers come face to face with ancient rituals, intricate art forms, and traditional music and dance that tell the island's stories and shape its identity. By observing or participating in these cultural practices, visitors gain a profound appreciation for Balinese values and beliefs. The culture, rooted deeply in Hinduism and philosophies like Tri Hita Karana—striving for harmony among people, nature, and the spiritual realm—encourages visitors to reflect on the balance in their own lives.

Experiencing life through the Balinese lens offers lessons in mindfulness, patience, and the importance of ritual. For instance, witnessing the daily offerings of canang sari (small floral offerings made to gods and spirits) reinforces the significance of gratitude and humility in even the simplest actions. These moments remind travellers to live with intention and presence, inspiring many to bring these mindful practices back home with them. The lessons drawn from Balinese customs and philosophies offer travellers a refreshing, holistic approach to life, helping them view challenges with a newfound sense of perspective.

Finding Inner Peace and Healing through Wellness: Bali is often described as a healing destination, a sanctuary where travellers come to reconnect with their inner selves and rediscover peace. The island's wellness retreats, yoga centers, and meditation spaces invite travellers to pause, rejuvenate, and focus on mental and physical well-being. For many, practicing yoga on an Ubud terrace overlooking verdant rice paddies, meditating in a serene bamboo retreat, or participating in a wellness workshop becomes a journey of self-healing. Bali's wellness offerings encourage travellers to adopt self-care practices, realign their priorities, and cultivate a lifestyle rooted in balance and mindfulness.

Many travellers report a transformative experience in Bali's wellness spaces, where the focus on mental and spiritual health is as important as physical wellness. Guided by skilled practitioners, travellers learn to reconnect with themselves, explore emotional blocks, and gain clarity on personal aspirations and challenges. Bali's emphasis on holistic well-being fosters an environment where self-discovery and healing become an integral part of the journey. These experiences leave travellers not only revitalized but also inspired to integrate these wellness practices into their daily lives.

Connecting with Bali's Warm and Welcoming People: The true essence of Bali lies in the warmth and hospitality of its people, who embody kindness, resilience, and a deep respect for their culture and environment. Conversations with locals—whether a farmer in the rice paddies, a craftsman in Ubud, or a young entrepreneur in Canggu—reveal the Balinese people's love for their heritage, a willingness to share their stories, and a genuine interest in connecting with travellers from all walks of life. These interactions are often the highlight of a journey, as travellers feel welcomed into the local community and gain a deeper, more personal understanding of Balinese life.

For many travellers, the connections they make with Balinese people become cherished memories that enrich their journey. Whether it's learning to cook a traditional dish with a family, exchanging smiles and stories with a temple guide, or sharing a meal with locals during a festival, these moments leave travellers with an appreciation for Balinese generosity and the simplicity of genuine human connection. The warmth of the Balinese people often touches travellers on a personal level, creating a sense of belonging and leaving a lasting impact that they carry with them long after their journey ends.

Reflecting on Sustainability and Responsible Travel: Bali's commitment to sustainable tourism resonates deeply with travellers, many of whom are inspired to adopt more eco-conscious and responsible practices after witnessing Bali's efforts to protect its environment. From participating in beach clean-ups to supporting eco-friendly accommodations and businesses, travellers often find themselves more mindful of their environmental impact and motivated to contribute positively to the places they visit. Bali's sustainable tourism model demonstrates that it's possible to balance travel with environmental and cultural preservation, inspiring visitors to adopt responsible practices both on the island and back home.

Reflecting on Bali's sustainable efforts also encourages travellers to reconsider their relationship with nature and consumption. Many visitors leave Bali with a heightened awareness of the importance of protecting natural resources, respecting wildlife, and supporting local communities. This awareness often translates into a more mindful approach to travel and consumption, inspiring travellers to make conscious choices that benefit the environment and local communities long after their journey in Bali.

Taking a Piece of Bali's Spirit Back Home: Perhaps the most profound impact of a journey to Bali is the way it lingers in the heart and mind long after departure. Travellers often find themselves reflecting on their Bali experiences, whether it's the breathtaking sunrise over Mount Batur, the serene moments spent in meditation, or the joyful interactions with Balinese locals. The lessons learned, the beauty witnessed, and the memories created in Bali leave an indelible mark, inspiring travellers to bring a piece of Bali's spirit into their everyday lives.

For many, this means adopting practices that echo Bali's values—living with mindfulness, respecting nature, valuing human connections, and finding joy in simple, intentional acts. Bali's influence often becomes a guiding force, shaping how travellers approach challenges, relationships, and personal growth. In this way, Bali's transformative power extends beyond the journey, becoming a lifelong source of inspiration and grounding.

Bali: A Journey that Transforms the Heart: In the end, a journey to Bali is a journey to the soul. It is a place that opens travellers to new perspectives, teaches valuable life lessons, and encourages a more meaningful connection with the world. Bali's beauty, culture, people, and traditions are not just elements of a destination; they are threads that weave into the traveller's own story, leaving them forever changed. For those who venture to Bali, the island becomes a part of them, a place they carry within, always reminding them to live with gratitude, joy, and respect for the world around them. In Bali, travellers discover not only the island's heart but their own as well, making it a journey that resonates long after they return home, and one that beckons them back time and time again.

* * *

Our Itinerary in Bali

Day 1 (March 6, 2024): Arrival in Bali

- Late Night Flight: Departed from Kolkata Airport; had a layover in Bangkok before reaching Denpasar, Bali.
- Arrival: Arrived in Bali during the early evening; greeted by a host holding a sign with our names.
- Car Rental: Picked up a white Toyota Agya rental and drove to our hotel in Kuta.
- Explored Kuta: Strolled through lively streets, sampled satay, and watched a mesmerizing sunset on Kuta Beach.

Day 2 (March 7, 2024): Sunrise at Tanah Lot & Uluwatu Temple

- Early Start: Woke at 4 a.m. and drove to Tanah Lot to witness a serene sunrise over the iconic ocean temple.
- Tanah Lot: Spent time filming, learning about the temple's significance, and interacting with locals.
- Uluwatu Temple: Drove to Uluwatu; admired the stunning cliffside views and filmed the breathtaking landscapes.
- Suluban Beach: Descended narrow steps to this hidden beach; met surfers and explored sea caves.
- Evening: Ended the day with a relaxing dinner at an open-air café in Kuta.

Day 3 (March 8, 2024): Handara Gate, Ulun Danu Beratan Temple, & Banyumala Waterfall

- Early Morning: Left for Handara Gate; captured iconic photos of the misty gateway and lush surroundings.
- Ulun Danu Beratan Temple: Visited this floating temple on Lake

Beratan, soaked in the serene ambiance, and witnessed local ceremonies.
- Banyumala Waterfall: Rented a motorbike to access the secluded waterfall; enjoyed its pristine beauty.
- Stay: Checked into an Airbnb in Kintamani overlooking Lake Batur and enjoyed a starry, tranquil evening.

Day 4 (March 9, 2024): Mount Batur Trek & Sideman
- Pre-Dawn Adventure: Started the trek at 2 a.m. with a guide; reached Mount Batur's summit for sunrise.
- Volcanic Ash Fields: Explored the ashen terrain surrounding Mount Batur.
- Kintamani Exploration: Spent the afternoon relaxing and soaking in views of the lake and mountains.

- Scenic Drive: Headed to Sideman, passing through terraced rice fields and traditional Balinese villages.
- Stay: Checked into a hillside Airbnb surrounded by greenery, hills, and waterfalls; spent a peaceful evening.

Day 5 (March 10, 2024): Lempuyang Temple & Virgin Beach
- Lempuyang Temple: Visited the famous Gates of Heaven with stunning views of Mount Agung.
- Virgin Beach: Relaxed on the tranquil white-sand beach and swam in the clear blue waters.

- Ogoh Ogoh Festival

Day 6 (March 11, 2024): Nyepi Eve

- Ogoh-Ogoh Festival: Witnessed vibrant parades and elaborately crafted statues celebrating Nyepi Eve.
- Stay: Spent a serene night in preparation for the Balinese Day of Silence.

Day 7 (March 12, 2024): Nusa Penida

- Early Ferry: Took a ferry from Sanur Port to Nusa Penida.
- Kelingking Beach: Admired the T-Rex-shaped cliffs and white sand beaches.
- Angel's Billabong & Broken Beach: Explored these natural formations and infinity pools.
- Crystal Bay: Watched a stunning sunset and relaxed on the beach.

Day 8 (March 13, 2024): Diamond Beach

- Morning Adventure: Hiked down to Diamond Beach, famous for its clear waters and limestone formations.
- Return to Bali: Took the ferry back to Bali in the evening; enjoyed a candlelit dinner at Sanur.

Day 9 (March 14, 2024): Departure

- Last Morning: Packed souvenirs and cherished the final moments in Bali.
- Flight Home: Departed from Denpasar with a heart full of memories.

Places That We Have Missed,

But You Should Go!

Bali, with its endless charm and diverse landscapes, is a treasure trove of destinations. While our journey was filled with unforgettable moments, there were several incredible places we didn't get the chance to visit but would wholeheartedly recommend to future travellers. These spots promise unique experiences, stunning views, and a deeper connection to Bali's culture and nature.

Sekumpul Waterfalls: Often referred to as Bali's most beautiful waterfall, Sekumpul is a breathtaking sight nestled in the northern part of the island. This hidden gem requires a bit of effort to reach, with a trek through lush forests and a series of steps leading down to the base. However, the journey is worth every step. Imagine standing before a towering cascade of seven waterfalls, each pouring into a serene pool below, surrounded by emerald-green cliffs. The cool mist of the water and the peaceful ambiance make this spot a haven for nature lovers and adventure seekers alike. It's an experience of pure tranquillity and raw beauty.

Sacred Monkey Forest in Ubud: This lush sanctuary in Ubud is home to hundreds of Balinese long-tailed monkeys. The Sacred Monkey Forest isn't just a popular tourist attraction; it's also an important spiritual and cultural site, housing ancient temples within its dense greenery. Walking through the forest feels like stepping into another world, where playful monkeys swing from the trees and ancient stone carvings seem to whisper stories of the past. It's a perfect mix of adventure, cultural insight, and a touch of mischief, thanks to the lively monkey residents.

Tegalalang Rice Terrace and Jatiluwih Rice Fields: While Bali's rice terraces are iconic, Tegalalang and Jatiluwih stand out as two of the most picturesque. Tegalalang, located near Ubud, is known for its dramatic, tiered design and the opportunity to walk through the lush paddies. The morning light here is magical, with the terraces shimmering in golden hues. Jatiluwih, a UNESCO World Heritage Site, offers a more expansive and tranquil experience. These sweeping rice fields are set against the backdrop of Mount Batukaru, providing a glimpse into Bali's agricultural heritage and a moment of serenity amidst its natural beauty.

Amed Beach: For those seeking a quieter coastal escape, Amed Beach is a dream come true. Located on Bali's eastern coast, this stretch of black volcanic sand offers a stark contrast to the island's busier beaches. The calm waters make it a paradise for snorkelling and diving, revealing vibrant coral reefs and marine life just beneath the surface. Amed's laid-back vibe and stunning views of Mount Agung in the distance make it a perfect getaway for anyone looking to unwind and explore Bali's underwater treasures.

Gili Islands: Just a short boat ride from Bali, the Gili Islands are a slice of paradise that feels worlds away. Comprised of three small islands—Gili Trawangan, Gili Air, and Gili Meno—each offers its own unique charm. Whether it's the lively nightlife of Gili Trawangan, the serene beaches of Gili Meno, or the balanced tranquillity of Gili Air, these islands are perfect for snorkelling, diving, and basking in pristine natural beauty. Crystal-clear waters, vibrant coral gardens, and a complete absence of motor vehicles make the Gili Islands an idyllic escape.

Bali Swings: For thrill-seekers and Instagram enthusiasts alike, the Bali Swings offer an exhilarating way to take in the island's lush beauty. Located amidst the tropical jungle, these swings are perched high above the treetops, providing breathtaking views of the surrounding valleys, rice terraces, and rivers. Swinging out into the air, with the wind rushing past and the world spread out below, is an unforgettable experience. It's equal parts adrenaline and awe, and the photos are bound to become cherished keepsakes.

Pantai Pasut: Pantai Pasut is a hidden gem on Bali's western coast, far removed from the crowds of Kuta and Seminyak. This serene black sand beach is perfect for quiet walks, sunset views, and moments of reflection. Its unique feature is a solitary palm tree that arches dramatically over the sand, creating an iconic silhouette against the ocean backdrop. The beach's peaceful ambiance and unspoiled beauty make it a wonderful spot for those looking to escape into Bali's more tranquil side.

Kecak Dance at Uluwatu: The Kecak Dance, performed at Uluwatu Temple, is a cultural experience like no other. Set against the dramatic backdrop of a cliff overlooking the ocean, the performance unfolds as the sun dips below the horizon, painting the sky in fiery colours. The dance tells the story of the Ramayana, accompanied by the rhythmic chanting of performers in a hypnotic chorus. The combination of the setting, the culture, and the energy of the performance creates an atmosphere that is both magical and deeply moving.

Though we didn't get to visit these places ourselves, each destination holds the promise of unforgettable experiences and the chance to uncover a different facet of Bali's magic. Whether it's the serenity of a hidden beach, the thrill of a jungle swing, or the cultural depth of an ancient dance, these spots invite you to explore, connect, and immerse yourself in the wonders of Bali. Add them to your itinerary, and let them enrich your journey in ways only this enchanting island can.

* * *

- THE END –

Author Biography

Shibjit Mitra, born on July 28, 1997, is an advocate practicing at the esteemed Calcutta High Court. With a foundation in technology through a Bachelor of Technology in Electronics and an LLB Honours degree, he skilfully balances his professional life with his creative passions.

Writing has been Shibjit's lifelong companion, nurtured since childhood by his mother's encouragement to weave stories and compose poems. Travel, too, became a cherished pursuit, sparking a dream to craft captivating travel narratives. With the unwavering support and inspiration of his wife, Krittika, Shibjit turned this dream into reality, blending his love for exploration and storytelling.

A dedicated traveller and vlogger, Shibjit's adventures reflect his zest for discovering the world and sharing its wonders. *Journey to The Sacred Island* marks his foray into publishing, offering readers a heartfelt tale that captures the beauty of exploration and the joy of storytelling.